WHERE IN THE WORLD ARE WE NOW?

NORTH AND SOUTH AMERICA ASIA EUROPE

By
Anthony Tallarico

AFRICA
AUSTRALIA
AND
ANTARCTICA

FILLED WITH FACTS

...AND FUN

kidsbooks
Incorporated

WHERE IN THE WORLD ARE WE NOW ?

ASIA, AUSTRALIA, and ANTARCTICA

By
Anthony Tallarico

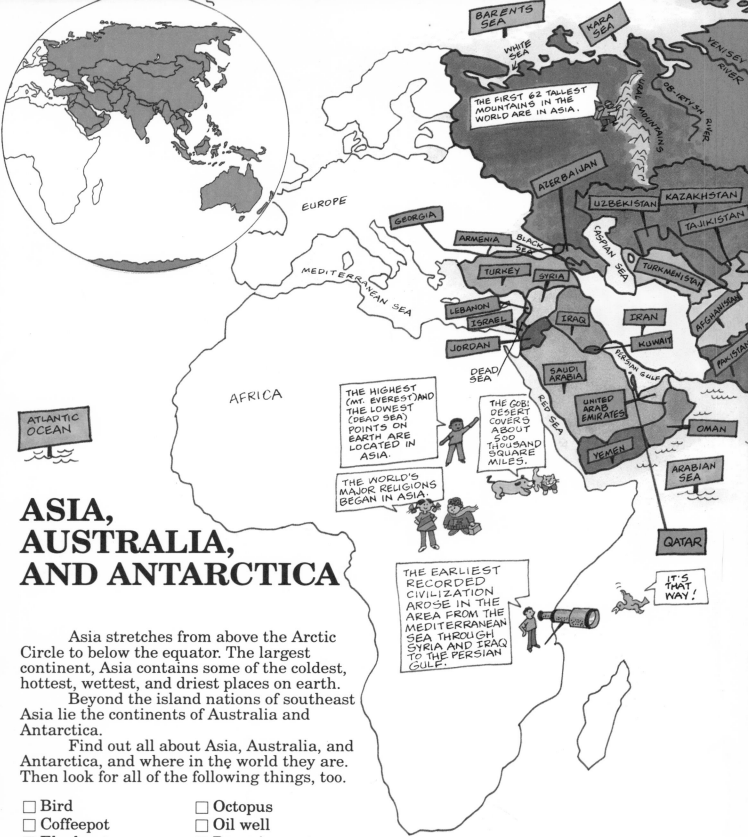

ASIA, AUSTRALIA, AND ANTARCTICA

Asia stretches from above the Arctic Circle to below the equator. The largest continent, Asia contains some of the coldest, hottest, wettest, and driest places on earth.

Beyond the island nations of southeast Asia lie the continents of Australia and Antarctica.

Find out all about Asia, Australia, and Antarctica, and where in the world they are. Then look for all of the following things, too.

- [ ] Bird
- [ ] Coffeepot
- [ ] Elephant
- [ ] Gold
- [ ] Kangaroo
- [ ] Lobster
- [ ] Mermaid
- [ ] Mountain climber
- [ ] Octopus
- [ ] Oil well
- [ ] Penguin
- [ ] Polar bear
- [ ] Sailboat
- [ ] Telescope

Labels on map: BARENTS SEA, KARA SEA, WHITE SEA, YENISEY RIVER, OB-IRTYSH RIVER, URAL MOUNTAINS, THE FIRST 62 TALLEST MOUNTAINS IN THE WORLD ARE IN ASIA., AZERBAIJAN, UZBEKISTAN, KAZAKHSTAN, TAJIKISTAN, EUROPE, GEORGIA, ARMENIA, BLACK SEA, CASPIAN SEA, TURKMENISTAN, TURKEY, SYRIA, MEDITERRANEAN SEA, LEBANON, ISRAEL, JORDAN, IRAQ, IRAN, KUWAIT, AFGHANISTAN, PAKISTAN, DEAD SEA, PERSIAN GULF, SAUDI ARABIA, UNITED ARAB EMIRATES, AFRICA, THE HIGHEST (MT. EVEREST) AND THE LOWEST (DEAD SEA) POINTS ON EARTH ARE LOCATED IN ASIA., THE GOBI DESERT COVERS ABOUT 500 THOUSAND SQUARE MILES., RED SEA, OMAN, ATLANTIC OCEAN, THE WORLD'S MAJOR RELIGIONS BEGAN IN ASIA., YEMEN, ARABIAN SEA, QATAR, THE EARLIEST RECORDED CIVILIZATION AROSE IN THE AREA FROM THE MEDITERRANEAN SEA THROUGH SYRIA AND IRAQ TO THE PERSIAN GULF., IT'S THAT WAY!

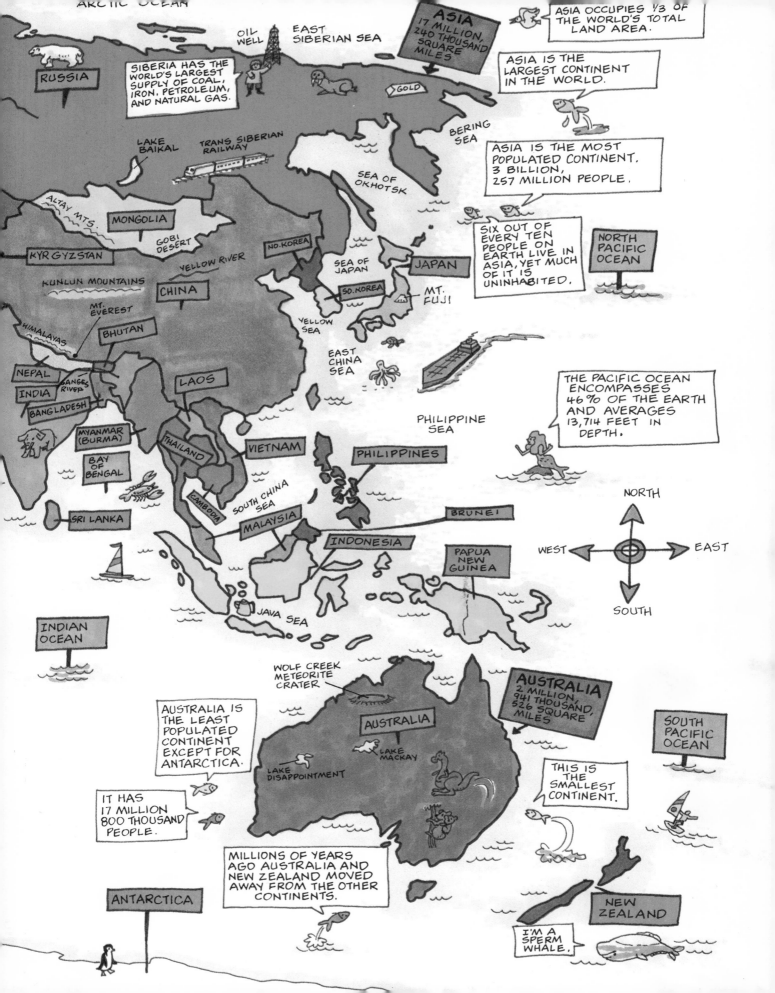

RUSSIA AND THE NEWLY INDEPENDENT ASIAN NATIONS

Russia, the world's largest country, lies in two continents — Asia and Europe. It stretches for 6,000 miles, covering more than half of Europe and more than 35% of Asia.

Russia used to be part of the USSR, or Soviet Union, which dissolved in 1991. The republics that made up the USSR, in both Europe and Asia, are now 15 independent countries. Eleven of them have formed an association called The Commonwealth of Independent States.

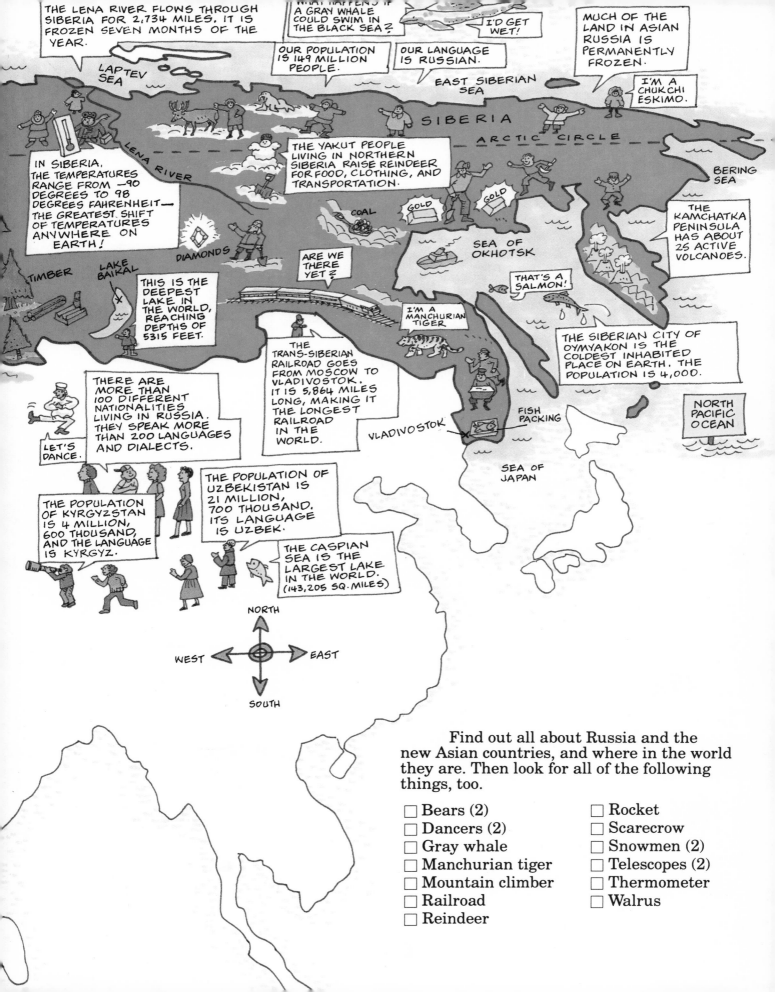

Find out all about Russia and the new Asian countries, and where in the world they are. Then look for all of the following things, too.

- ☐ Bears (2)
- ☐ Dancers (2)
- ☐ Gray whale
- ☐ Manchurian tiger
- ☐ Mountain climber
- ☐ Railroad
- ☐ Reindeer
- ☐ Rocket
- ☐ Scarecrow
- ☐ Snowmen (2)
- ☐ Telescopes (2)
- ☐ Thermometer
- ☐ Walrus

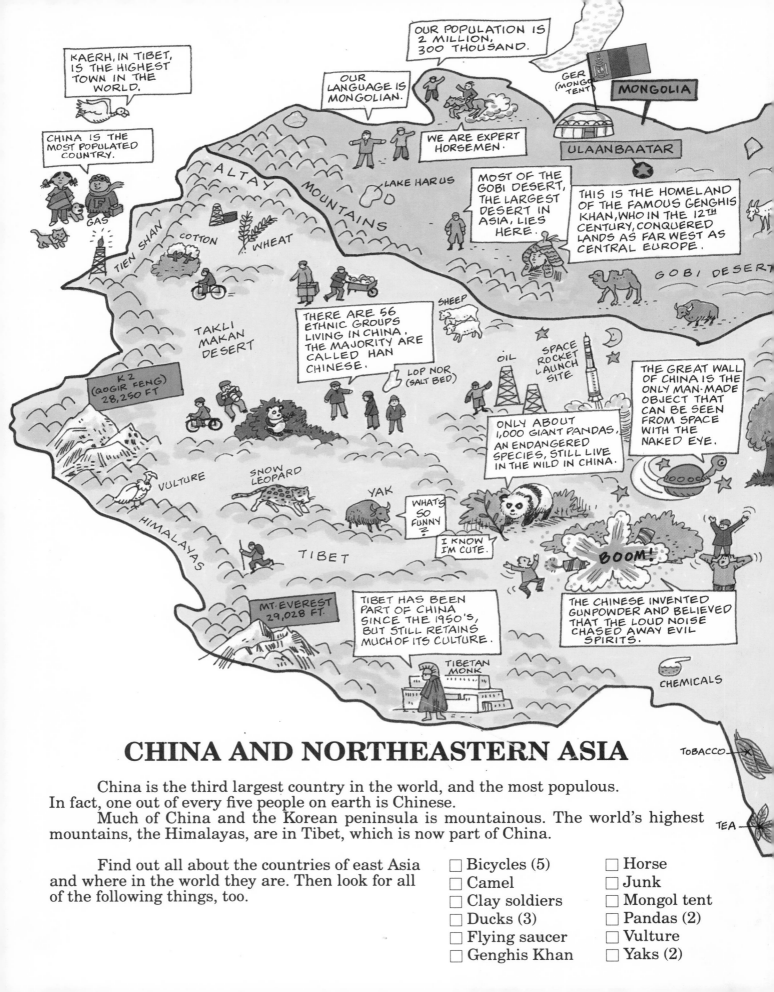

CHINA AND NORTHEASTERN ASIA

China is the third largest country in the world, and the most populous. In fact, one out of every five people on earth is Chinese.

Much of China and the Korean peninsula is mountainous. The world's highest mountains, the Himalayas, are in Tibet, which is now part of China.

Find out all about the countries of east Asia and where in the world they are. Then look for all of the following things, too.

- ☐ Bicycles (5)
- ☐ Camel
- ☐ Clay soldiers
- ☐ Ducks (3)
- ☐ Flying saucer
- ☐ Genghis Khan
- ☐ Horse
- ☐ Junk
- ☐ Mongol tent
- ☐ Pandas (2)
- ☐ Vulture
- ☐ Yaks (2)

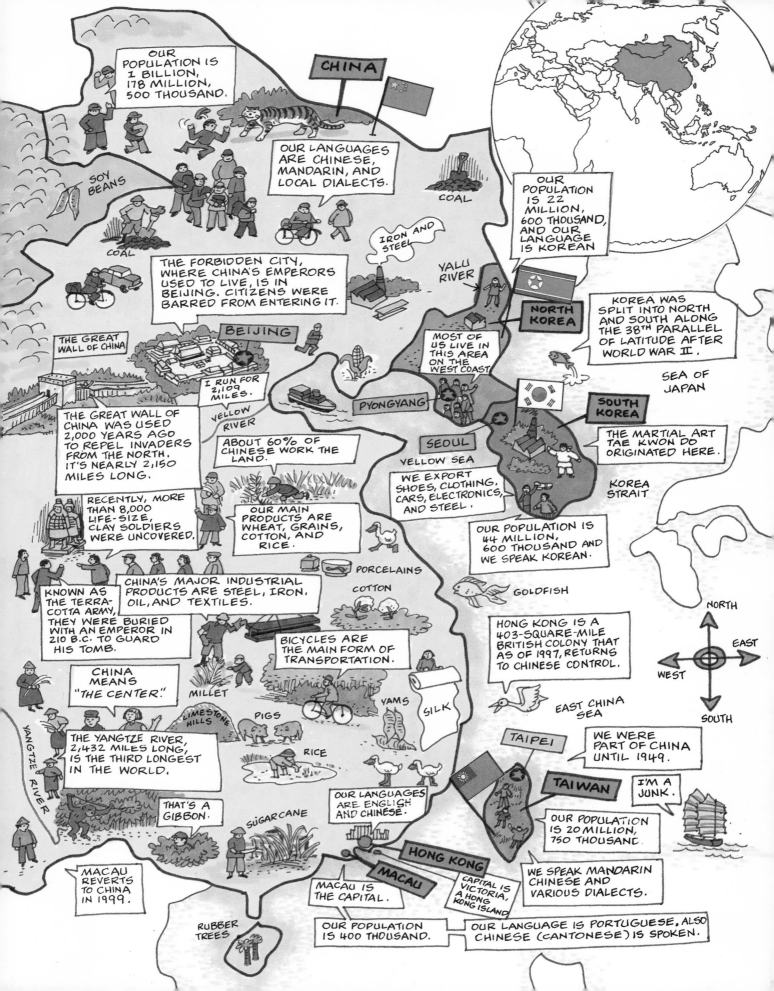

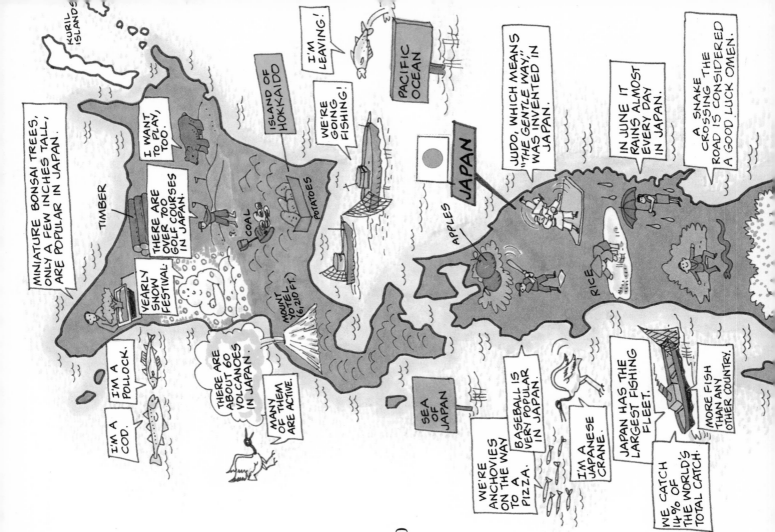

JAPAN

Japan consists of four main islands and about 4,000 smaller ones. This densely populated and leading industrial country is almost as large as California. Most of the people live in the big cities on Honshu Island and along the flat coastal areas.

Find out all about Japan and where in the world it is. Then look for all of the following things, too.

- ☐ Anchovies
- ☐ Baseball bat
- ☐ Brown bear
- ☐ Cod
- ☐ Cook
- ☐ Crab
- ☐ Cranes (2)
- ☐ Dollar sign
- ☐ Golfer
- ☐ Octopus
- ☐ Skier
- ☐ Snake
- ☐ Snow sculpture
- ☐ Squid
- ☐ Streamer
- ☐ Tofu
- ☐ Turtle
- ☐ Umbrellas (2)
- ☐ Wrestler

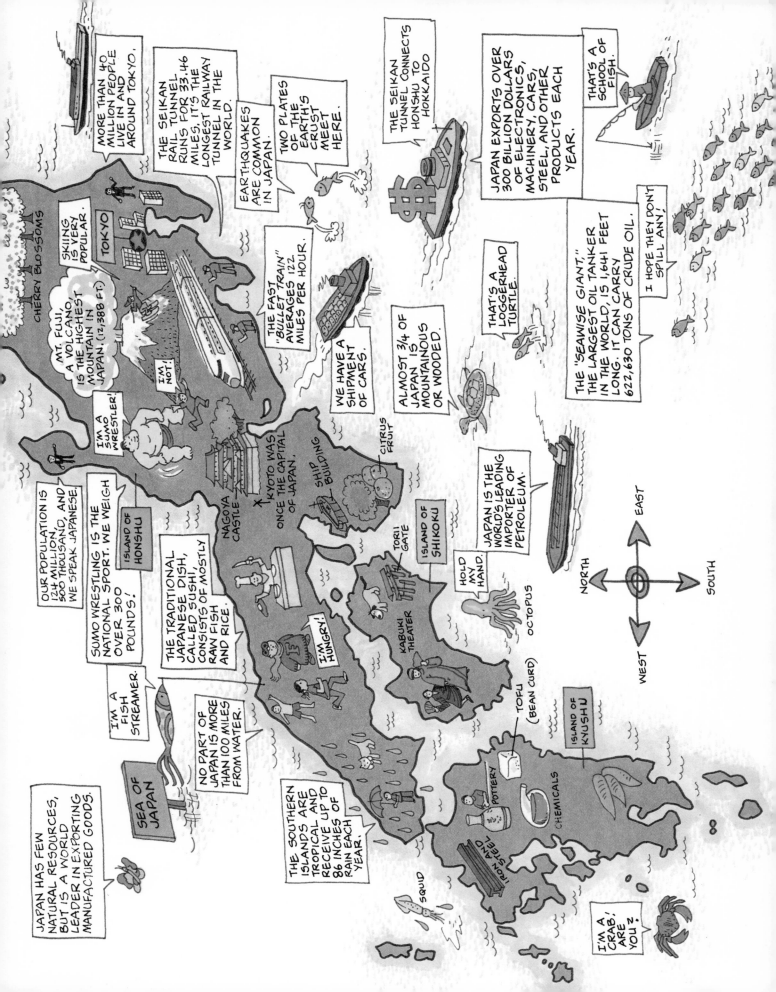

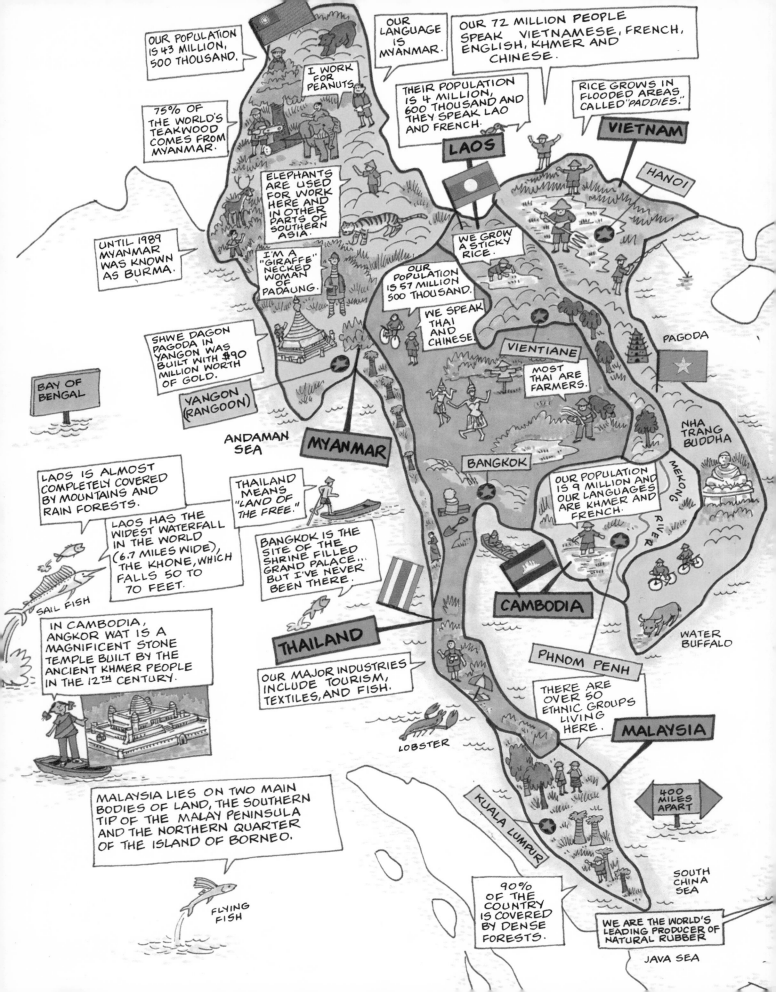

SOUTHEAST ASIA

Much of this region is covered with jungles, mountains, and rain forests. The Mekong River, 2,600 miles long, is the longest river in southeast Asia. It begins in the Himalayan Mountains, flows through five countries, and empties into the South China sea. Fifty million people depend on the river for irrigation, fish, and transportation.

Find out all about the countries of Southeast Asia and where in the world they are. Then look for all of the following things, too.

- ☐ Brown bears (2)
- ☐ Cyclists (3)
- ☐ Dancers
- ☐ Deer
- ☐ Elephant
- ☐ Fisherman
- ☐ Flying fish
- ☐ "Giraffe" neck
- ☐ Lobster
- ☐ Pitchfork
- ☐ Scarecrow
- ☐ Tiger
- ☐ Umbrellas (2)

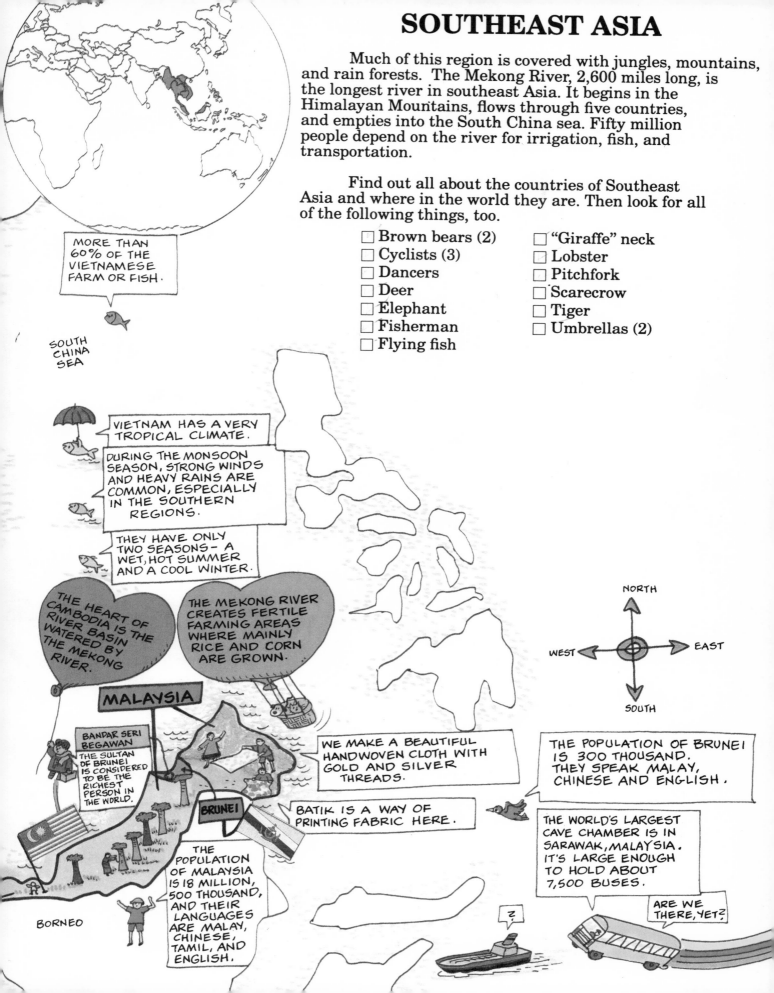

MORE THAN 60% OF THE VIETNAMESE FARM OR FISH.

SOUTH CHINA SEA

VIETNAM HAS A VERY TROPICAL CLIMATE.

DURING THE MONSOON SEASON, STRONG WINDS AND HEAVY RAINS ARE COMMON, ESPECIALLY IN THE SOUTHERN REGIONS.

THEY HAVE ONLY TWO SEASONS— A WET, HOT SUMMER AND A COOL WINTER.

THE HEART OF CAMBODIA IS THE RIVER BASIN WATERED BY THE MEKONG RIVER.

THE MEKONG RIVER CREATES FERTILE FARMING AREAS WHERE MAINLY RICE AND CORN ARE GROWN.

MALAYSIA

BANDAR SERI BEGAWAN

THE SULTAN OF BRUNEI IS CONSIDERED TO BE THE RICHEST PERSON IN THE WORLD.

BRUNEI

THE POPULATION OF MALAYSIA IS 18 MILLION, 500 THOUSAND, AND THEIR LANGUAGES ARE MALAY, CHINESE, TAMIL, AND ENGLISH.

BORNEO

WE MAKE A BEAUTIFUL HANDWOVEN CLOTH WITH GOLD AND SILVER THREADS.

BATIK IS A WAY OF PRINTING FABRIC HERE.

NORTH
WEST — EAST
SOUTH

THE POPULATION OF BRUNEI IS 300 THOUSAND. THEY SPEAK MALAY, CHINESE AND ENGLISH.

THE WORLD'S LARGEST CAVE CHAMBER IS IN SARAWAK, MALAYSIA. IT'S LARGE ENOUGH TO HOLD ABOUT 7,500 BUSES.

ARE WE THERE, YET?

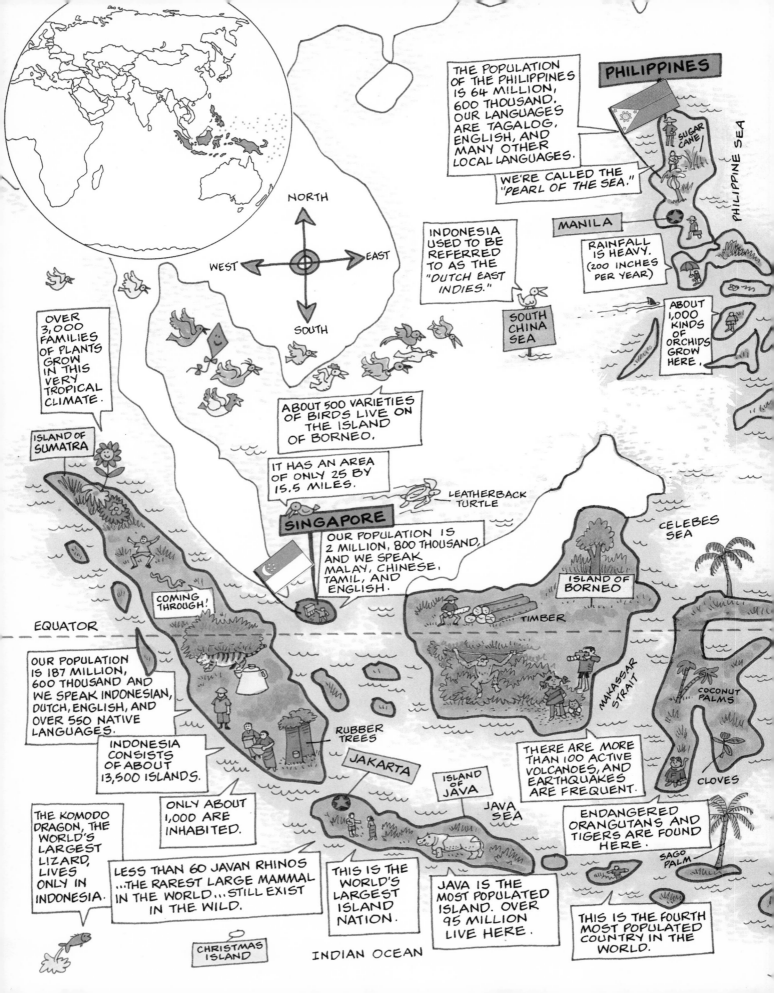

INDONESIA AND THE ISLAND NATIONS

The island nations of Southeastern Asia were an important source of spices for the Europeans, who fought to control the spice trade. The region was once known as the East Indies.

The islands receive lots of rain during the monsoon season. The climate in this heavily forested land is hot and sticky most of the year.

Find out all about Indonesia and the island nations, and where in the world they are. Then look for all of the following things, too.

☐ Airplane   ☐ Kite   ☐ Rhinoceros   ☐ Tiger
☐ Coffeepot ☐ Orangutan   ☐ Shark fins (4) ☐ Turtle
☐ Kangaroo   ☐ Photographer ☐ Snakes (2)   ☐ Volcanoes (2)

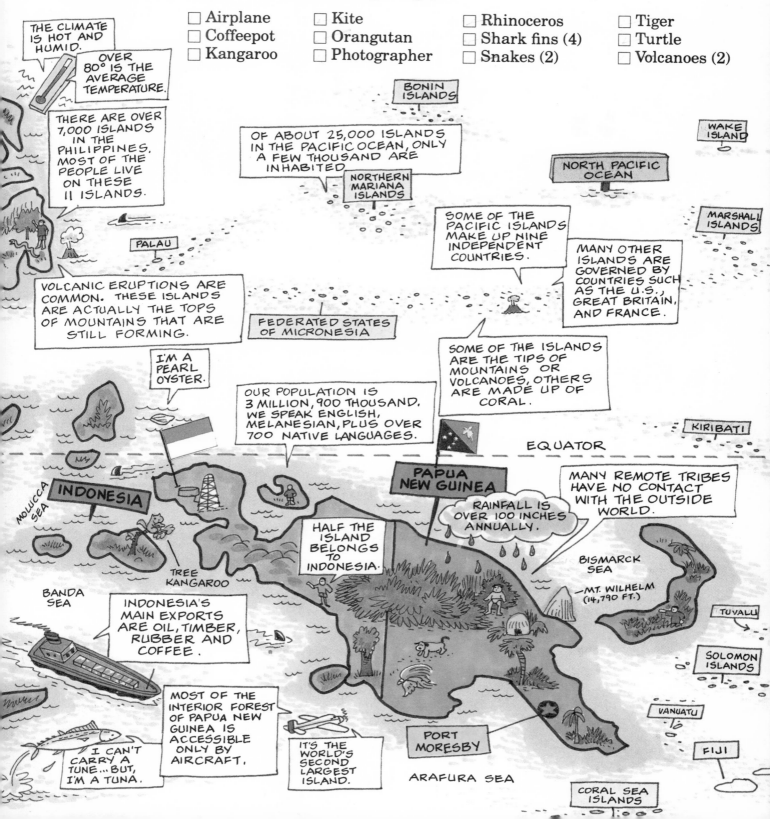

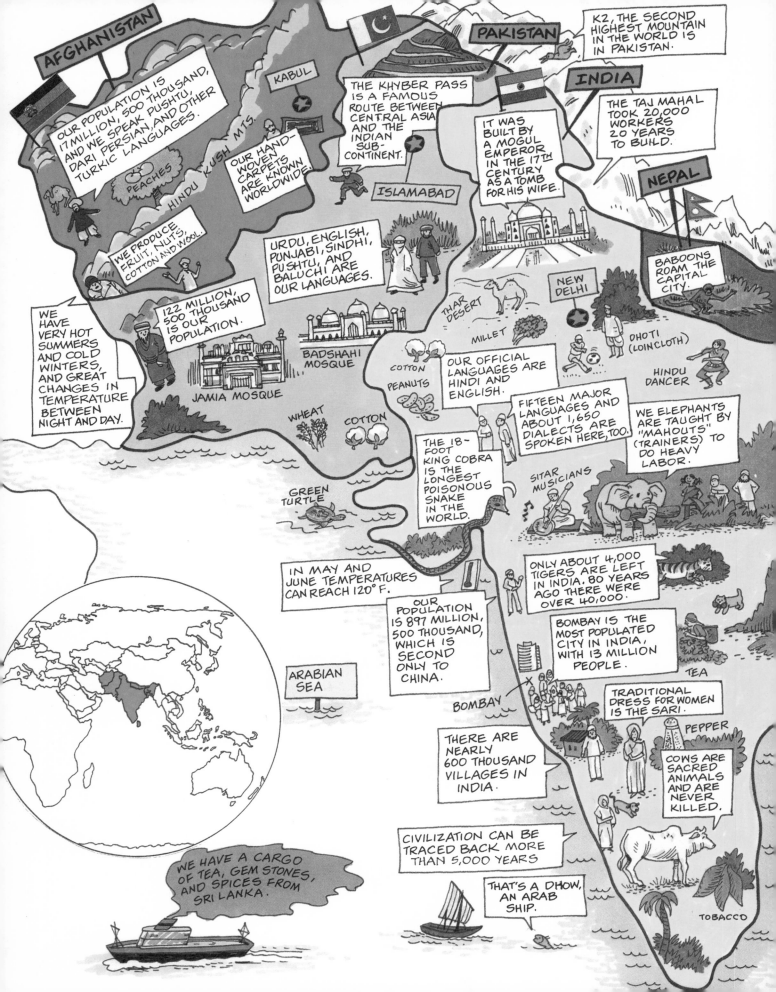

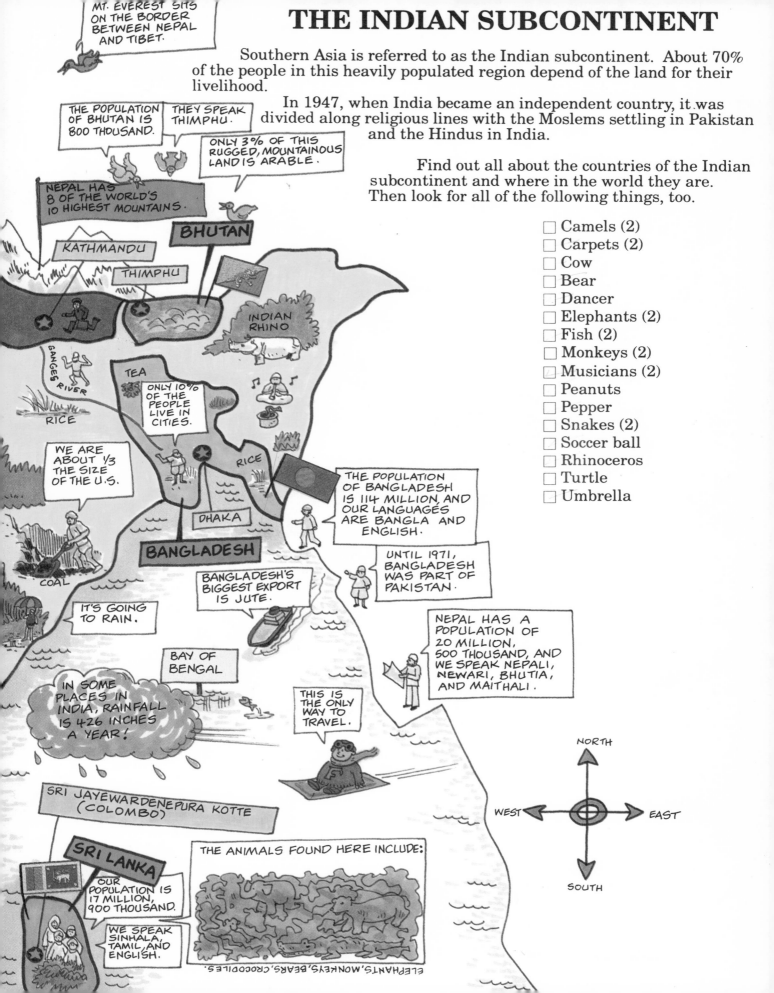

THE INDIAN SUBCONTINENT

MT. EVEREST SITS ON THE BORDER BETWEEN NEPAL AND TIBET.

Southern Asia is referred to as the Indian subcontinent. About 70% of the people in this heavily populated region depend of the land for their livelihood.

In 1947, when India became an independent country, it was divided along religious lines with the Moslems settling in Pakistan and the Hindus in India.

Find out all about the countries of the Indian subcontinent and where in the world they are. Then look for all of the following things, too.

THE POPULATION OF BHUTAN IS 800 THOUSAND.

THEY SPEAK THIMPHU.

ONLY 3% OF THIS RUGGED, MOUNTAINOUS LAND IS ARABLE.

NEPAL HAS 8 OF THE WORLD'S 10 HIGHEST MOUNTAINS.

☐ Camels (2)
☐ Carpets (2)
☐ Cow
☐ Bear
☐ Dancer
☐ Elephants (2)
☐ Fish (2)
☐ Monkeys (2)
☑ Musicians (2)
☐ Peanuts
☐ Pepper
☐ Snakes (2)
☑ Soccer ball
☐ Rhinoceros
☐ Turtle
☐ Umbrella

BHUTAN

KATHMANDU

THIMPHU

INDIAN RHINO

GANGES RIVER

TEA

ONLY 10% OF THE PEOPLE LIVE IN CITIES.

RICE

WE ARE ABOUT 1/3 THE SIZE OF THE U.S.

RICE

THE POPULATION OF BANGLADESH IS 114 MILLION, AND OUR LANGUAGES ARE BANGLA AND ENGLISH.

DHAKA

BANGLADESH

UNTIL 1971, BANGLADESH WAS PART OF PAKISTAN.

COAL

BANGLADESH'S BIGGEST EXPORT IS JUTE.

IT'S GOING TO RAIN.

NEPAL HAS A POPULATION OF 20 MILLION, 500 THOUSAND, AND WE SPEAK NEPALI, NEWARI, BHUTIA, AND MAITHALI.

BAY OF BENGAL

IN SOME PLACES IN INDIA, RAINFALL IS 426 INCHES A YEAR!

THIS IS THE ONLY WAY TO TRAVEL.

NORTH
WEST EAST
SOUTH

SRI JAYEWARDENEPURA KOTTE (COLOMBO)

SRI LANKA

OUR POPULATION IS 17 MILLION, 900 THOUSAND.

THE ANIMALS FOUND HERE INCLUDE:

WE SPEAK SINHALA, TAMIL, AND ENGLISH.

ELEPHANTS, MONKEYS, BEARS, CROCODILES.

THE MIDDLE EAST

One of the first places where civilization was recorded is in the area between the Tigris and Euphrates rivers. Towns and communities were thriving here 6,000 years ago. Today, the region produces about 1/3 of the world's petroleum.

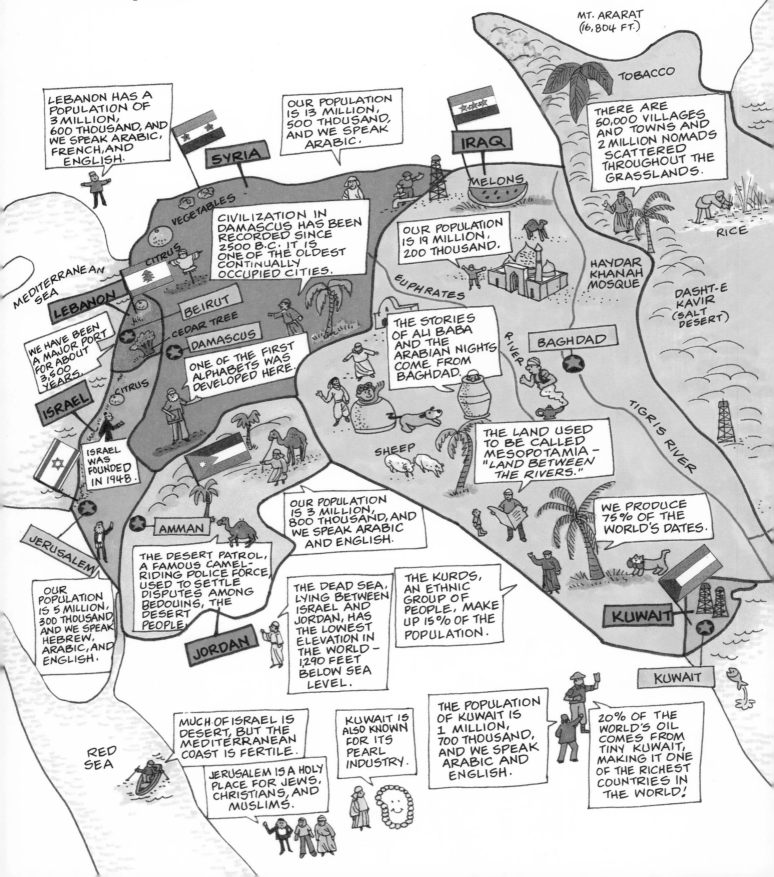

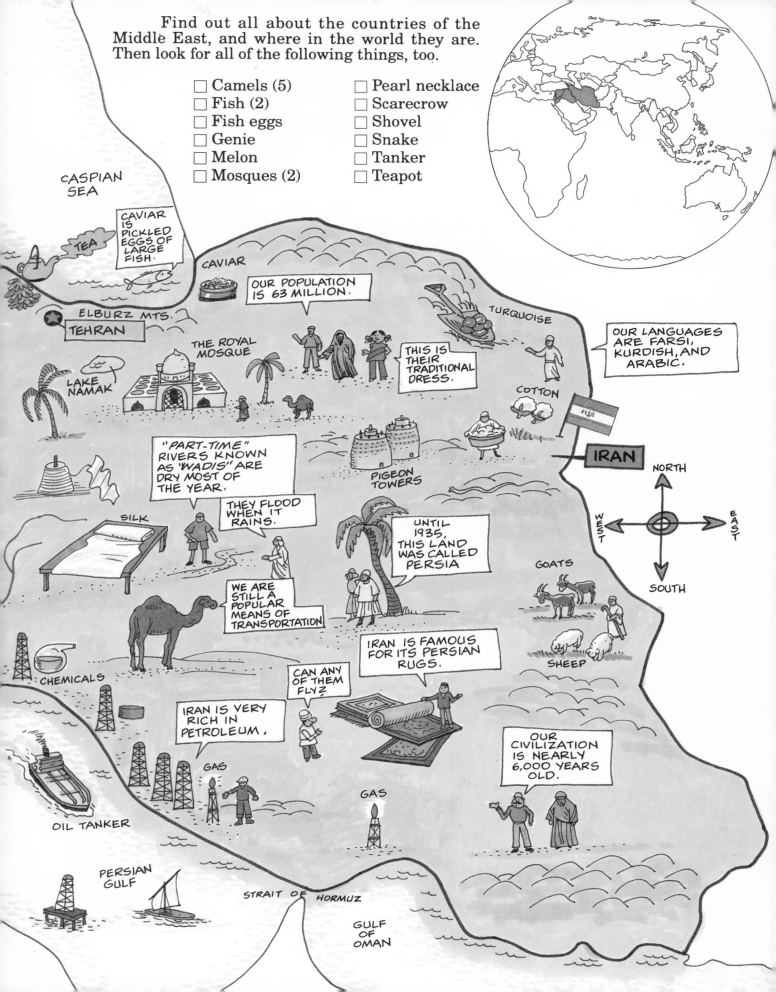

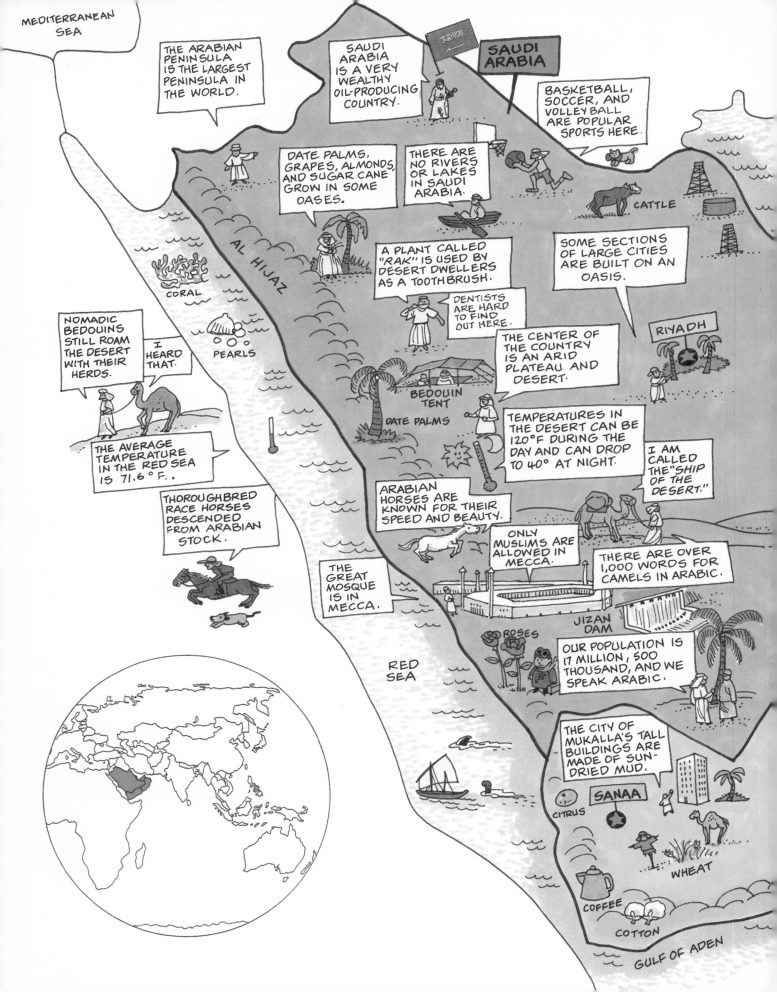

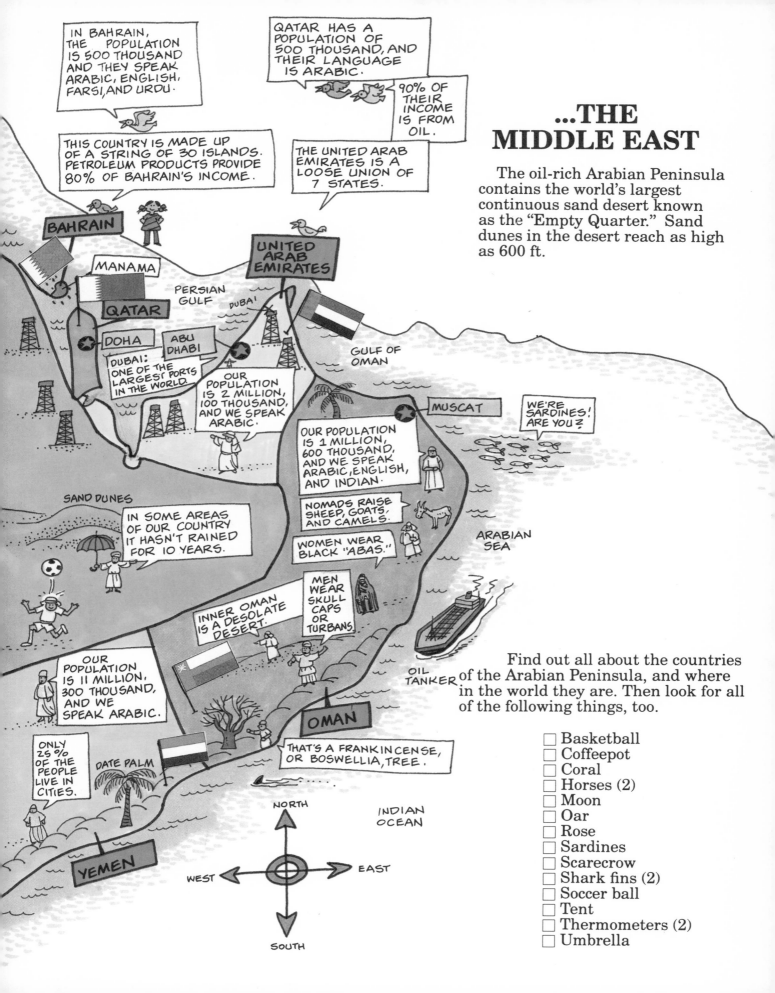

...THE MIDDLE EAST

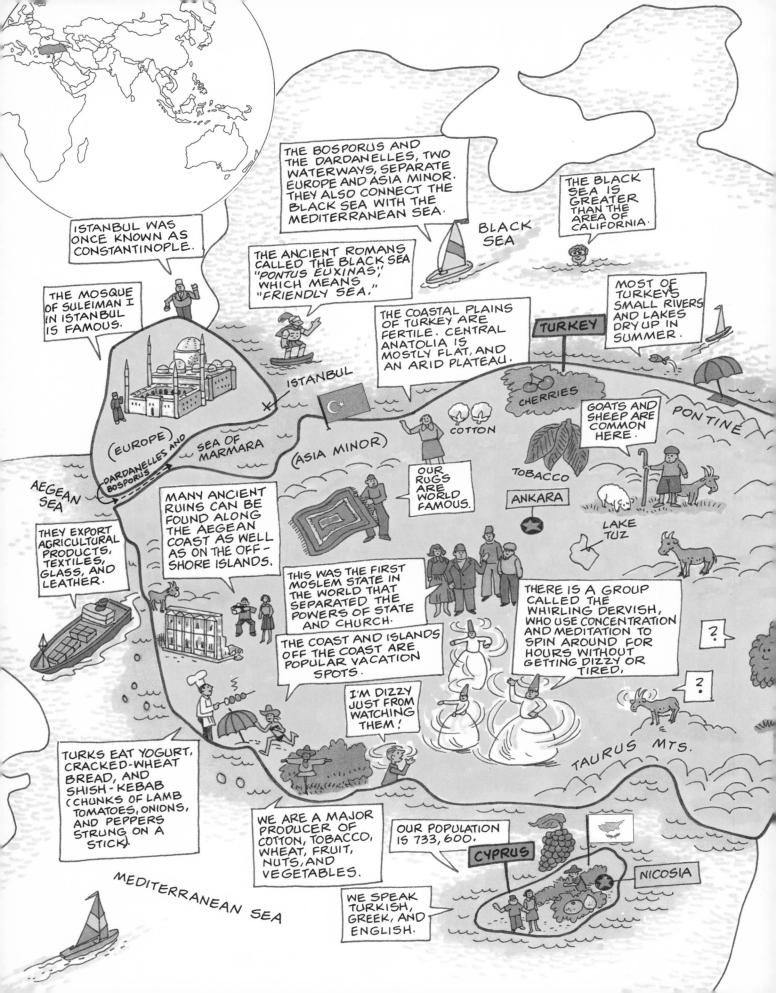

TURKEY AND CYPRUS

Three percent of Turkey lies in Europe. The rest is in Asia and is called Anatolia or Asia Minor. Istanbul is Turkey's largest city and the only city in the world that occupies land on two continents.

Find out all about Turkey and Cyprus, and where in the world they are. Then look for all of the following things, too.

- ☐ Apples
- ☐ Ball
- ☐ Bears (3)
- ☐ Book
- ☐ Cook
- ☐ Egg
- ☐ Fish
- ☐ Goats (5)
- ☐ Grapes
- ☐ Ibis
- ☐ Ladder
- ☐ Sailboats (3)
- ☐ Shepherd
- ☐ Tea bag
- ☐ Telescope
- ☐ Texan
- ☐ Tin man
- ☐ Umbrellas (2)

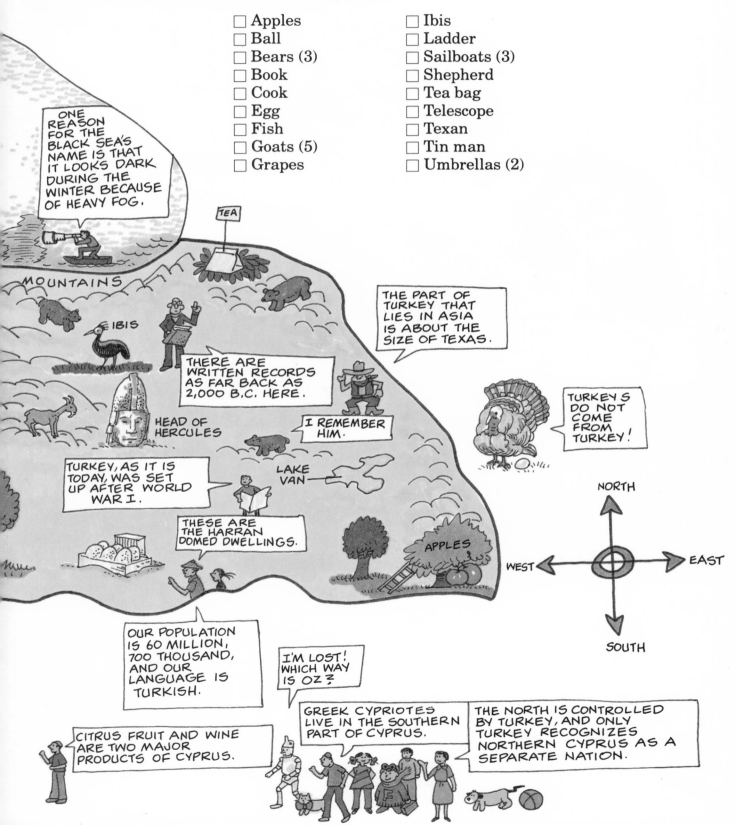

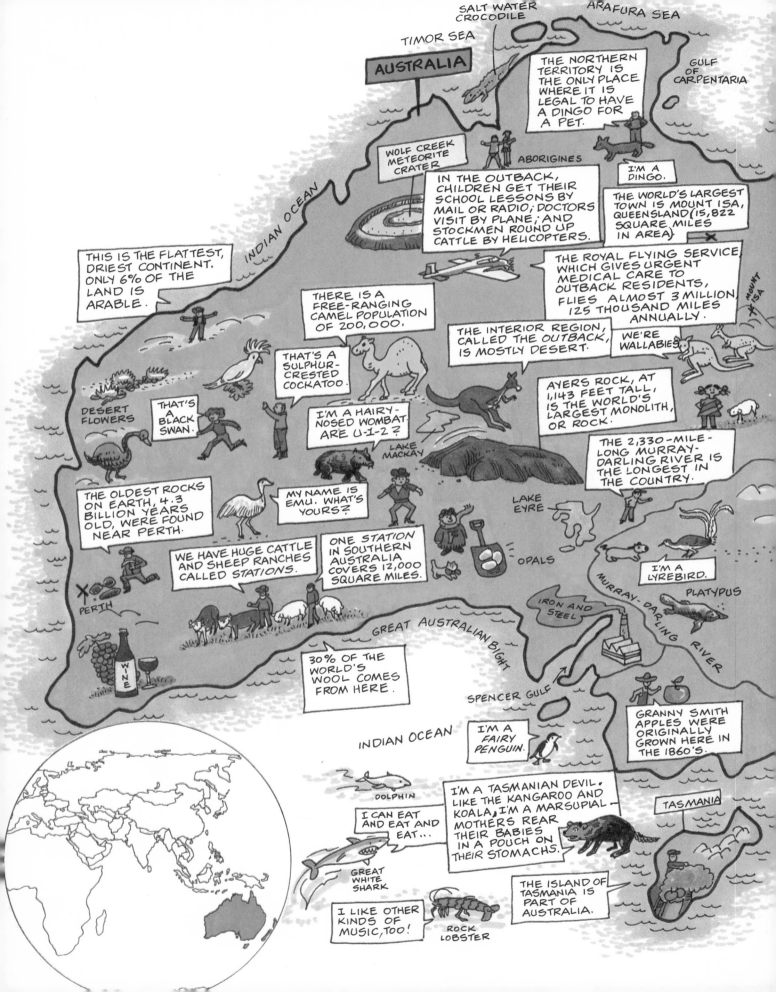

AUSTRALIA AND NEW ZEALAND

Australia is the only country in the world to occupy an entire continent. It's called "Down Under" because the whole country lies south of the equator.

Millions of years ago Australia separated from the other continents. The first settlers were the Aborigines, who came from islands in the Pacific Ocean about 40,000 years ago.

Find out all about Australia and New Zealand, and where in the world they are. Then look for all of the following things, too.

- ☐ Banana
- ☐ Camel
- ☐ Cockatoo
- ☐ Emu
- ☐ Kangaroo
- ☐ Koalas (2)
- ☐ Lyrebird
- ☐ Penguin
- ☐ Platypus
- ☐ Sharks (2)
- ☐ Skier
- ☐ Surfers (2)
- ☐ Swan
- ☐ Tasmanian devil
- ☐ Volcano
- ☐ Wallabies (2)
- ☐ Wombat

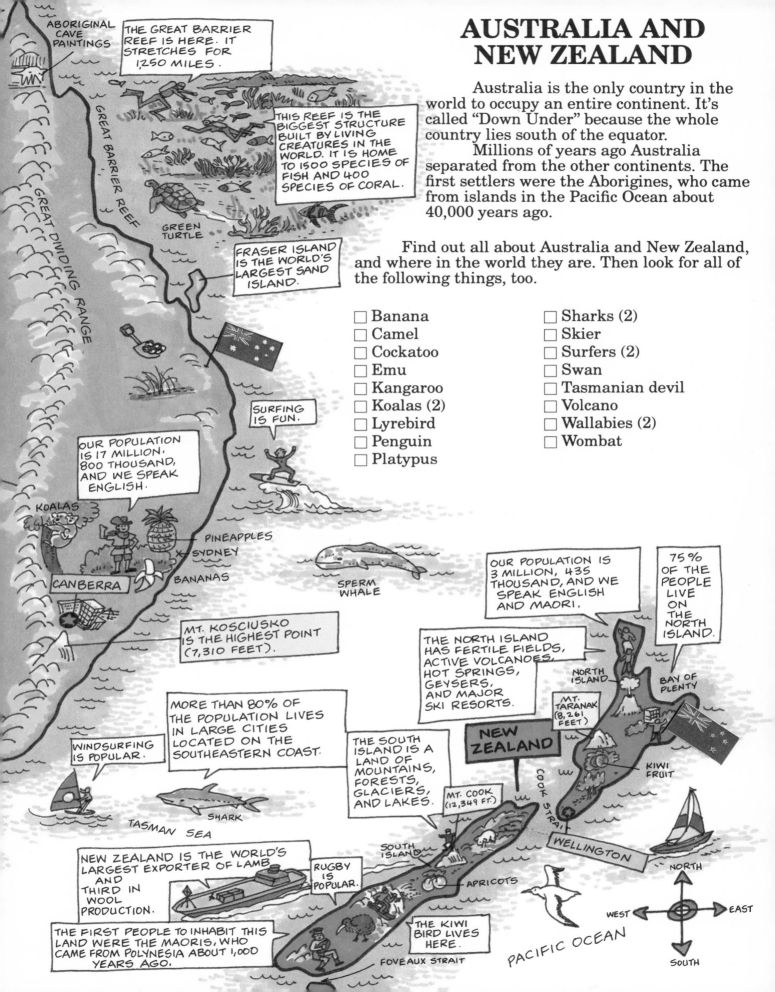

ABORIGINAL CAVE PAINTINGS

THE GREAT BARRIER REEF IS HERE. IT STRETCHES FOR 1,250 MILES.

THIS REEF IS THE BIGGEST STRUCTURE BUILT BY LIVING CREATURES IN THE WORLD. IT IS HOME TO 1500 SPECIES OF FISH AND 400 SPECIES OF CORAL.

GREAT BARRIER REEF

GREAT DIVIDING RANGE

GREEN TURTLE

FRASER ISLAND IS THE WORLD'S LARGEST SAND ISLAND.

SURFING IS FUN.

OUR POPULATION IS 17 MILLION, 800 THOUSAND, AND WE SPEAK ENGLISH.

KOALAS

PINEAPPLES

SYDNEY

CANBERRA

BANANAS

SPERM WHALE

MT. KOSCIUSKO IS THE HIGHEST POINT (7,310 FEET).

OUR POPULATION IS 3 MILLION, 435 THOUSAND, AND WE SPEAK ENGLISH AND MAORI.

75% OF THE PEOPLE LIVE ON THE NORTH ISLAND.

THE NORTH ISLAND HAS FERTILE FIELDS, ACTIVE VOLCANOES, HOT SPRINGS, GEYSERS, AND MAJOR SKI RESORTS.

NORTH ISLAND

BAY OF PLENTY

MT. TARANAK (8,261 FEET)

NEW ZEALAND

KIWI FRUIT

MORE THAN 80% OF THE POPULATION LIVES IN LARGE CITIES LOCATED ON THE SOUTHEASTERN COAST.

WINDSURFING IS POPULAR.

THE SOUTH ISLAND IS A LAND OF MOUNTAINS, FORESTS, GLACIERS, AND LAKES.

MT. COOK (12,349 FT.)

COOK STRAIT

SHARK

TASMAN SEA

WELLINGTON

NEW ZEALAND IS THE WORLD'S LARGEST EXPORTER OF LAMB AND THIRD IN WOOL PRODUCTION.

RUGBY IS POPULAR.

SOUTH ISLAND

APRICOTS

NORTH

THE FIRST PEOPLE TO INHABIT THIS LAND WERE THE MAORIS, WHO CAME FROM POLYNESIA ABOUT 1,000 YEARS AGO.

THE KIWI BIRD LIVES HERE.

WEST EAST

FOVEAUX STRAIT

PACIFIC OCEAN

SOUTH

ANTARCTICA

Antarctica is the coldest place on earth, with temperatures as low as -125°F. Although it is larger than the United States, no one owns it. Only scientific research bases are there.

Find out all about Antarctica and where in the world it is.
Then look for all of the following things, too.

- ☐ Baby penguin
- ☐ Dinosaur
- ☐ Elephant seals (:
- ☐ Lost mitten
- ☐ Snowman
- ☐ Snowmobile
- ☐ Whales (3)

INDIAN OCEAN

TO AFRICA

ANTARCTICA

SOUTH PACIFIC OCEAN

TO AUSTRALIA

ANTARCTIC PENINSULA

BELLINGSHAUSEN SEA

AMUNDSEN SEA

ROSS SEA

ROSS ICE SHELF

ICE BREAKER

HUMPBACK WHALE

WEDDELL SEA

RONNE ICE SHELF

FILCHNER ICE SHELF

AMERY ICE SHELF

SOUTH ATLANTIC OCEAN

SOUTH POLE

McMURDO AIR STATION (U.S.A.)

KRILL

FISH FACTORY SHIP

KILLER WHALE

ICE FISH

BLUE WHALE

TOURIST SHIP

THIS IS A NICE PLACE TO VISIT BUT I WOULDN'T WANT TO LIVE HERE!

THE SOUTH POLE, UNLIKE THE NORTH POLE, IS LOCATED ON A SOLID MASS OF LAND.

I'M AN ANTARCTIC PETREL.

THERE ARE AT LEAST 100 MILLION PENGUINS HERE.

THE HIGHEST POINT HERE IS THE VINSON MASSIF -16,864 FEET HIGH.

IN 1991, FOSSILS WERE FOUND OF A MEAT-EATING DINOSAUR THAT ROAMED HERE 200 MILLION YEARS AGO.

WHERE'S YOUR COAT?

THERE ARE FIVE VOLCANOES IN ANTARCTICA.

IT NEVER RAINS HERE.

IT'S COLD HERE.

I'M C-COLD!

WHAT'S "RAIN"?

DID YOU SEE HIM, MAMA?

IF ALL THE ICE MELTED, THE SEAS THROUGHOUT THE WORLD WOULD RISE 200 FEET!

THERE IS MORE FRESH WATER IN THE FORM OF ICE HERE THAN IN ALL THE REST OF THE WORLD.

THE CONTINENT IS COMPLETELY COVERED WITH ICE. IN SOME PLACES THE ICE IS 6,500 FEET THICK!

IN 1911, ROALD AMUNDSEN, A NORWEGIAN EXPLORER, WAS THE FIRST PERSON TO REACH THE SOUTH POLE.

THAT ELEPHANT SEAL SHOULD KNOW.

THERE ARE SIX MONTHS OF CONTINUOUS DAYLIGHT, THEN SIX MONTHS OF CONTINUOUS DARKNESS.

WHERE IN THE WORLD ARE WE NOW ?

EUROPE

By
Anthony Tallarico

kidsbooks Incorporated

Copyright © 1994 Kidsbooks, Inc. and Anthony Tallarico
3535 West Peterson Avenue
Chicago, IL 60659

EUROPE

The seat of western civilization, Europe has had a strong influence on the world through trade, exploration, and industry.

The continent stretches from the icy Arctic Circle in the north to the warm Mediterranean Sea in the south. The land, with its great fertile plains and tall mountains, is as varied as its people and the countries it contains.

Find out all about the countries of Europe, and where in the world they are. Then look for all of the following things, too.

- ☐ Cyclist
- ☐ Eiffel Tower
- ☐ Fish (3)
- ☐ Grapes
- ☐ Puffin
- ☐ Sailboat
- ☐ Volcano
- ☐ Windmill
- ☐ Wooden shoe

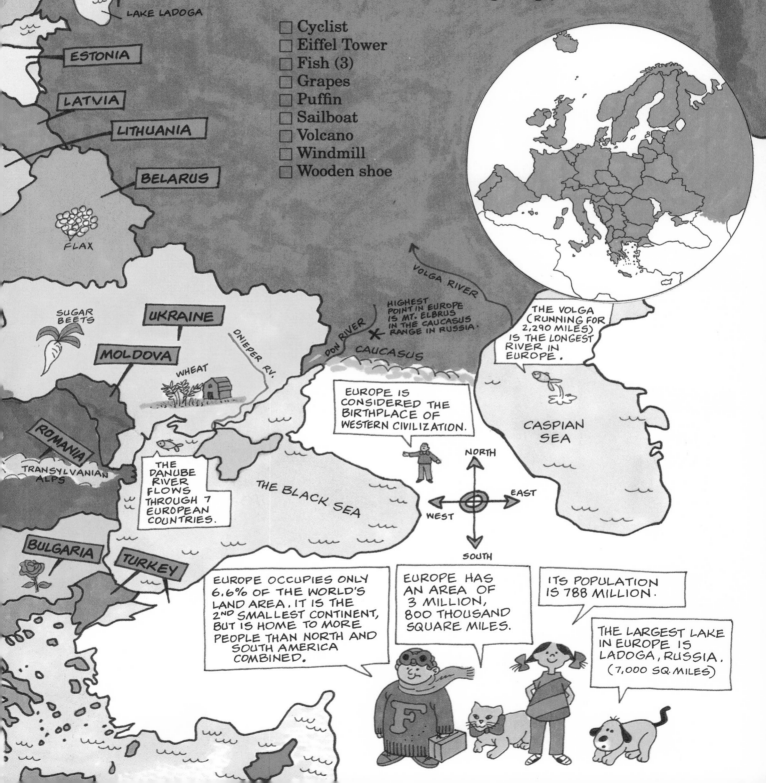

FINLAND

RUSSIA

LAKE LADOGA

ESTONIA

LATVIA

LITHUANIA

BELARUS

FLAX

SUGAR BEETS

UKRAINE

MOLDOVA

WHEAT

DNIEPER RV.

ROMANIA

TRANSYLVANIAN ALPS

BULGARIA

TURKEY

VOLGA RIVER

DON RIVER

HIGHEST POINT IN EUROPE IS MT. ELBRUS IN THE CAUCASUS RANGE IN RUSSIA.

CAUCASUS

THE VOLGA (RUNNING FOR 2,290 MILES) IS THE LONGEST RIVER IN EUROPE.

CASPIAN SEA

EUROPE IS CONSIDERED THE BIRTHPLACE OF WESTERN CIVILIZATION.

THE DANUBE RIVER FLOWS THROUGH 7 EUROPEAN COUNTRIES.

THE BLACK SEA

NORTH

WEST   EAST

SOUTH

EUROPE OCCUPIES ONLY 6.6% OF THE WORLD'S LAND AREA. IT IS THE 2ND SMALLEST CONTINENT, BUT IS HOME TO MORE PEOPLE THAN NORTH AND SOUTH AMERICA COMBINED.

EUROPE HAS AN AREA OF 3 MILLION, 800 THOUSAND SQUARE MILES.

ITS POPULATION IS 788 MILLION.

THE LARGEST LAKE IN EUROPE IS LADOGA, RUSSIA. (7,000 SQ. MILES)

The British Isles

The British Isles are made up of two countries, Ireland and the United Kingdom, also known as Great Britain. The United Kingdom consists of England, Scotland, Wales, and Northern Ireland.

In the 18th century Great Britain was the world's leading industrial and trading nation. Its worldwide empire included Canada, India, Australia, New Zealand, and parts of Africa. Today, 50 former colonies are part of the British Commonwealth of Nations.

Find out all about Ireland and the United Kingdom, and where in the world they are. Then look for all of the following things, too.

- ☐ Bagpipe
- ☐ "Big Ben"
- ☐ Bus
- ☐ Clock
- ☐ Cricket
- ☐ Crystal
- ☐ Deer
- ☐ Ferry
- ☐ Four-leaf clover
- ☐ Golf
- ☐ Knight in armor
- ☐ Lobster
- ☐ "Nessie"
- ☐ Sheep (3)
- ☐ Soccer ball
- ☐ Stonehenge
- ☐ Student
- ☐ Tennis racket

SHETLAND ISLANDS

HOME OF THE SHETLAND PONY

BAA.

SEALS

ORKNEY ISLANDS

NORTH SEA

UNITED KINGDOM OF GREAT BRITAIN

THERE ARE HUGE OIL AND NATURAL GAS RESERVES IN THE NORTH SEA.

BALMORAL CASTLE

SCOTLAND

THAT'S THE MYTHICAL LOCH (LAKE) NESS MONSTER.

BEN NEVIS 4,406 FEET - HIGHEST MOUNTAIN.

HELLO, I'M "NESSIE."

RED DEER

GLASGOW IS BRITAIN'S GREATEST INDUSTRIAL CENTER.

EDINBURGH

HOME OF THE BAGPIPE

HOME OF HARRIS TWEED

OUTER HEBRIDES

INNER HEBRIDES

NORTH UIST

SOUTH UIST

BAA.

SHIP BUILDING

WHEN IRELAND BECAME INDEPENDENT FROM BRITAIN IN 1921, NORTHERN IRELAND CHOSE TO REMAIN A PART OF THE UNITED KINGDOM.

NORTHERN IRELAND

BELFAST

TEXTILES - LACE

OUR POPULATION IS 3 MILLION, 521 THOUSAND, AND WE SPEAK IRISH (GAELIC) AND ENGLISH.

ATLANTIC OCEAN

DONEGAL BAY

POTATOES

IRELAND

THE IRISH LEGEND OF THE BLARNEY STONE SAYS THAT ANYONE WHO KISSES IT RECEIVES THE GIFT OF GAB.

Scandinavia

The countries of Denmark, Finland, Sweden, Norway, and Iceland make up the region known as Scandinavia. Many of the people here are descendants of the seafaring Vikings, who lived here about 1,000 years ago. Rich in natural resources, Scandinavians enjoy one of the highest living standards in the world.

Find out all about the countries of Scandinavia, and where in the world they are. Then look for all of the following things, too.

- ☐ Axe
- ☐ Birch tree
- ☐ Chef
- ☐ Dynamite
- ☐ Elk
- ☐ Flowers (2)
- ☐ Geyser
- ☐ "Legos"
- ☐ Lynx
- ☐ Pig
- ☐ Puffin
- ☐ Scarecrow
- ☐ Sheep (2)
- ☐ Skiers (2)
- ☐ Tepee
- ☐ Viking
- ☐ Volcanoes (2)
- ☐ Wolf

NORTH
EAST
WEST
SOUTH

MOST OF NORTHERN EUROPE IS FLAT, EXCEPT FOR THE MOUNTAINOUS SCANDINAVIAN COUNTRIES.

GULF OF FINLAND

HELSINKI

ICE-BREAKER SHIP

STOCKHOLM

GOTLAND

OLAND

BALTIC SEA

THIS IS THE HOME OF SMORGASBORD... A MEAL CONSISTING OF MANY DIFFERENT HOT AND COLD DISHES.

WE EXPORT MACHINERY, AUTOS, WOOD AND PAPER PRODUCTS, AND PETROLEUM.

LAKE VATTERN

LAKE VANERN

VOLVO AUTOS

OUR POPULATION IS 5 MILLION 163 THOUSAND, AND WE SPEAK DANISH.

KATTEGAT

COPENHAGEN

THE LITTLE MERMAID STATUE IS HERE.

IN 1792, DENMARK BECAME THE FIRST EUROPEAN STATE TO ABOLISH SLAVE TRADING.

OSLO

BAA!

LEGOLAND

DENMARK

SKAGERRAK

NORTH SEA

OUR CHIEF AGRICULTURAL EXPORTS ARE DAIRY PRODUCTS AND HAMS.

THERE ARE NO MOUNTAINS IN DENMARK.

THE DANES PERFECTED THE FIRST DIESEL ENGINE AND, IN 1912, LAUNCHED THE FIRST OCEANGOING MOTOR SHIP IN THE WORLD.

WE PLANT OVER 100,000 SAPLINGS EACH YEAR TO MAINTAIN OUR FORESTS.

The Iberian Peninsula

Spain and Portugal share a piece of land called the Iberian Peninsula. Both countries have a long seafaring history. Their explorers and settlers came to rule empires in Africa, Asia, and North and South America.

Today, fishing, farming, and tourism are major industries in both countries. More than 60 million tourists each year visit the historical cities and sun-drenched beaches of Spain and Portugal.

Find out all about Spain and Portugal, and where in the world they are. Then look for all of the following things, too.

- ☐ Anchovies
- ☐ Bottles (5)
- ☐ Brown bear
- ☐ Bulls (3)
- ☐ Car
- ☐ Cheese
- ☐ Cork
- ☐ Guitar
- ☐ Ibex
- ☐ Olive tree
- ☐ Skier
- ☐ Sunflowers (4)
- ☐ Umbrellas (3)
- ☐ Windmill
- ☐ Windsurfers (3)

WE ARE 4TH IN EUROPE IN AUTO MANUFACTURING.

WHERE'S MY CAR?

I DON'T DRIVE!

PORT WINE COMES FROM THE CITY OF PORTO.

GRAIN

POTATOES

FISH PROCESSING

BULLS ARE FOUGHT ON HORSEBACK AND ARE NOT KILLED IN PORTUGAL

SOCCER AND BULLFIGHTING ARE POPULAR HERE.

PORTUGAL

THE TAGUS RIVER DIVIDES THE COUNTRY IN TWO.

TAGUS RIVER

PORTUGAL IS THE WESTERNMOST COUNTRY IN EUROPE.

LISBON

20% OF THE POPULATION LIVES IN LISBON.

CITRUS FRUIT

GUADIANA RIVER

70% OF THE WORLD'S CORK COMES FROM HERE.

CORK

ATLANTIC OCEAN

AZORES (PORTUGAL)

OUR POPULATION IS 10 MILLION, 448 THOUSAND, AND WE SPEAK PORTUGUESE.

OLIVES

MADEIRA (PORTUGAL)

GUADALQUIVIR RIVER

WE ARE THE THIRD LARGEST COUNTRY IN EUROPE.

THE SPANISH PEOPLE HAVE MANY REGIONAL DIFFERENCES DUE TO THE SEPARATION BROUGHT ABOUT BY THE MOUNTAIN RANGES.

VASCO DE GAMA, IN 1497, WAS THE FIRST PERSON TO SAIL AROUND THE TIP OF AFRICA.

FERDINAND MAGELLAN WAS THE FIRST TO SAIL AROUND THE WORLD.

SHERRY WINE

I'M LATE FOR SCHOOL.

CANARY ISLANDS (SPAIN)

NORTH

EAST

WEST

SPAIN'S NATURAL MINERAL RESOURCES INCLUDE IRON, COAL, ZINC, AND URANIUM.

TALLEST MOUNTAIN IN SPAIN, PICO DE TEIDE. (12,188 FEET)

STRAIT OF GIBRALTAR

GIBRALTAR (2 3/4 MILES LONG AND RISES TO 1,394 FEET)

THE AVERAGE YEARLY RAINFALL IN SPAIN IS 20 INCHES —THE LOWEST IN WESTERN EUROPE.

ALBORAN SEA

SOUTH

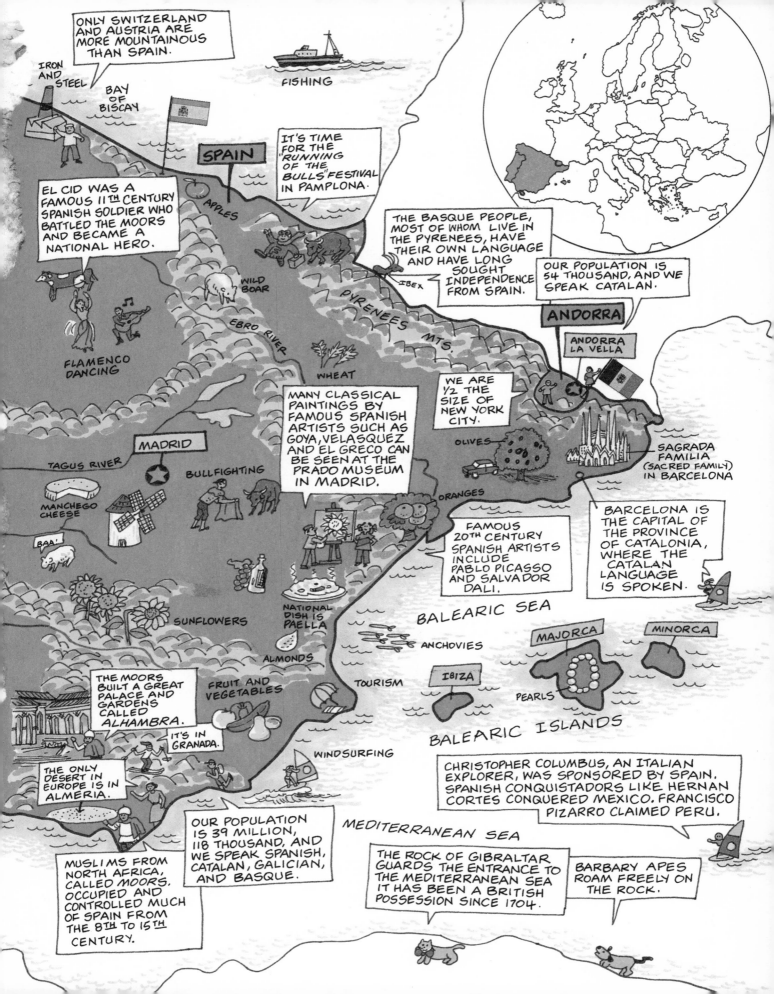

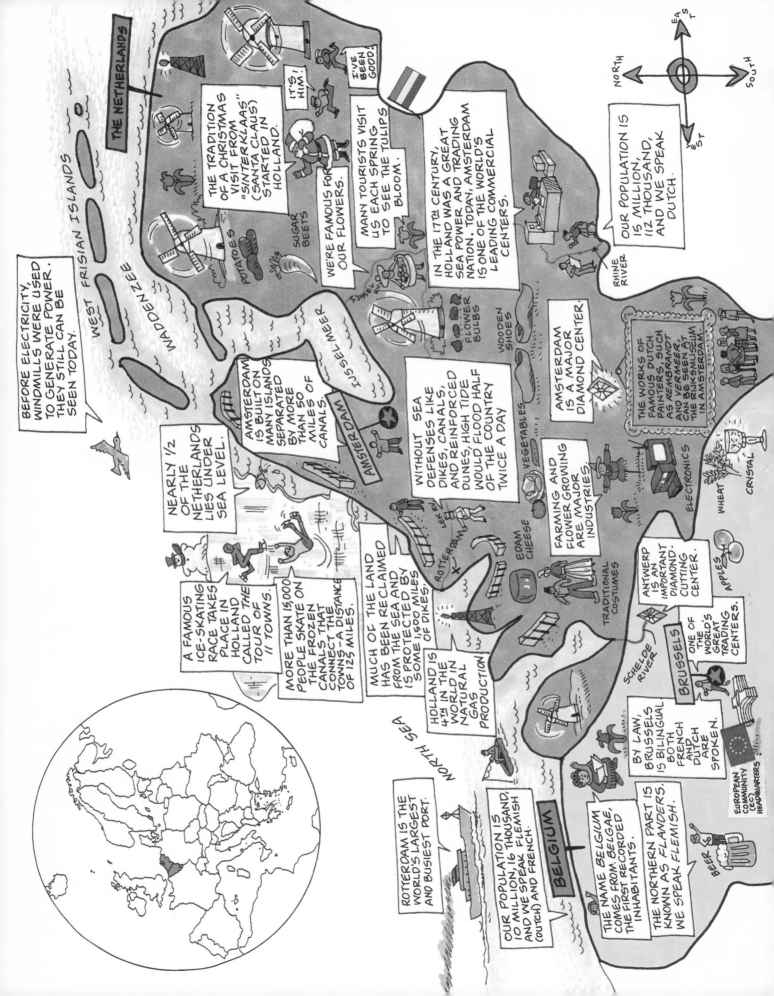

The Low Countries and Luxembourg

The Netherlands (also called Holland) and Belgium are situated on very low-lying land. Netherlands means "the lowlands," and with an average altitude of only 37 feet, it's the flattest country in the world.

Along with Luxembourg, these countries are sometimes referred to as "Benelux." Their small size and large populations make this region one of the most densely populated in Europe.

Find out all about the Low Countries and Luxembourg, and where in the world they are. Then look for all of the following things, too.

- ☐ Crystal
- ☐ Deer
- ☐ Diamonds (2)
- ☐ Fishing pole
- ☐ Frame
- ☐ Grapes
- ☐ Pig
- ☐ Santa Claus
- ☐ Shovel
- ☐ Telescope
- ☐ Tulips (5)
- ☐ TV set
- ☐ Waffle
- ☐ Windmills (5)
- ☐ Wooden shoes (2 pairs)

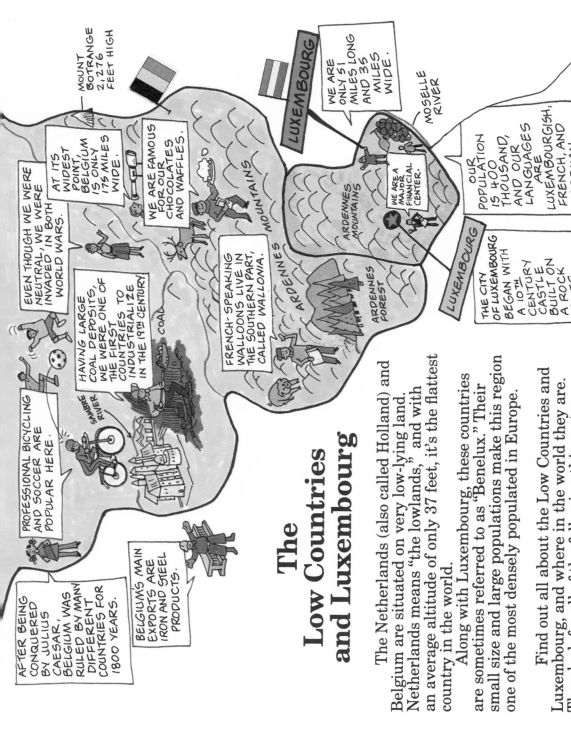

MOUNT BOTRANGE 2,276 FEET HIGH

LUXEMBOURG

WE ARE ONLY 51 MILES LONG AND 35 MILES WIDE.

MOSELLE RIVER

AT ITS WIDEST POINT, BELGIUM IS ONLY 175 MILES WIDE.

WE ARE FAMOUS FOR OUR CHOCOLATES AND WAFFLES.

OUR POPULATION IS 400 THOUSAND, AND OUR LANGUAGES ARE LUXEMBOURGISH, FRENCH, AND GERMAN.

EVEN THOUGH WE WERE NEUTRAL, WE WERE INVADED IN BOTH WORLD WARS.

MOUNTAINS

ARDENNES MOUNTAINS

WE ARE A MAJOR FINANCIAL CENTER.

LUXEMBOURG

THE CITY OF LUXEMBOURG BEGAN WITH A 10TH CENTURY CASTLE BUILT ON A ROCK CLIFF.

HAVING LARGE COAL DEPOSITS, WE WERE ONE OF THE FIRST COUNTRIES TO INDUSTRIALIZE IN THE 19TH CENTURY.

COAL

FRENCH-SPEAKING WALLOONS LIVE IN THE SOUTHERN PART, CALLED WALLONIA.

ARDENNES

ARDENNES FOREST

SAMBRE RIVER

PROFESSIONAL BICYCLING AND SOCCER ARE POPULAR HERE.

AFTER BEING CONQUERED BY JULIUS CAESAR, BELGIUM WAS RULED BY MANY DIFFERENT COUNTRIES FOR 1800 YEARS.

BELGIUM'S MAIN EXPORTS ARE IRON AND STEEL PRODUCTS.

France

France is the third largest country in Europe and the third oldest in the world. It is also one of the world's leading industrial and agricultural nations.

Paris is an international cultural center. The city is the site at which the French Revolution began in 1789, when France overthrew its king and declared itself a Republic.

Find out all about France, and where in the world it is. Then look for all of the following things, too.

☐ Apples (2)
☐ Artichoke
☐ Artist
☐ Automobile
☐ Chef
☐ Cyclist
☐ Dice
☐ Eels
☐ Eiffel Tower
☐ Geese (2)
☐ Mouse
☐ Musician
☐ Mustard
☐ Napoleon
☐ Paper airplane
☐ Perfume bottle
☐ Pig
☐ Red balloon
☐ Skier
☐ Snail
☐ Soccer ball
☐ Umbrellas (2)
☐ Walnuts

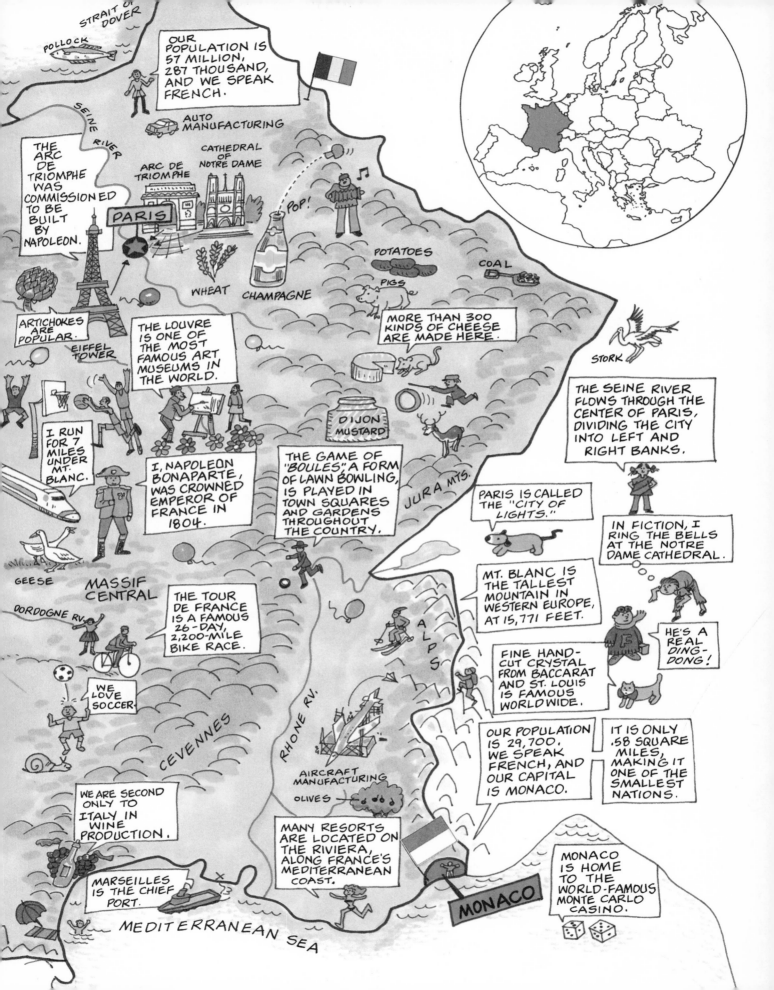

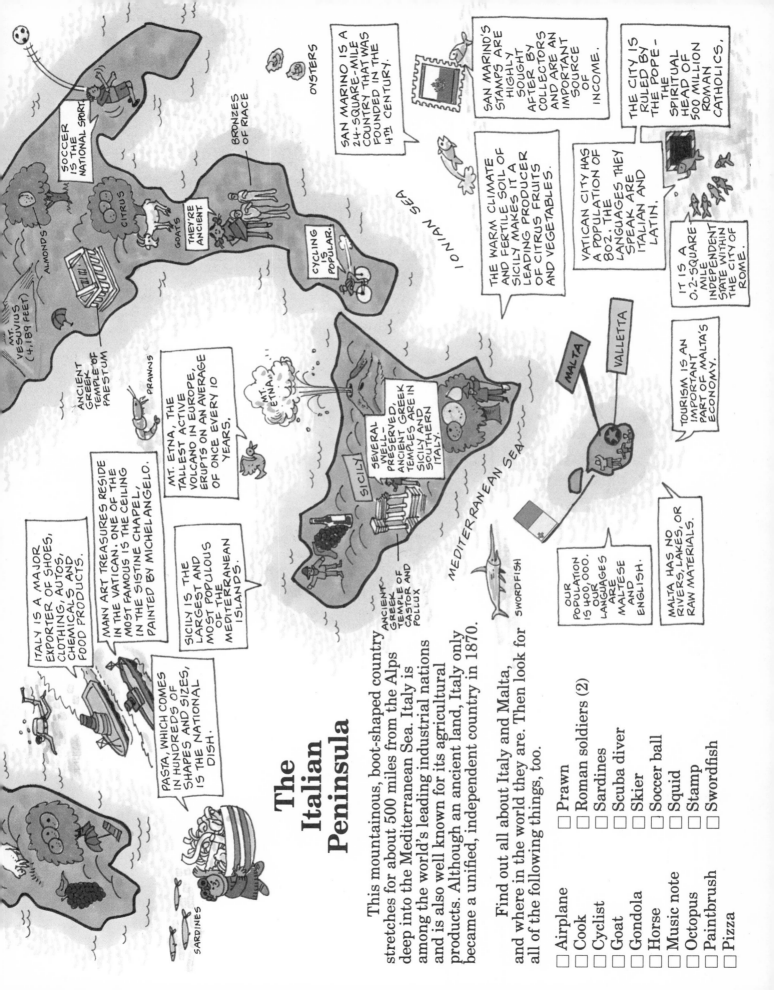

The Italian Peninsula

This mountainous, boot-shaped country stretches for about 500 miles from the Alps deep into the Mediterranean Sea. Italy is among the world's leading industrial nations and is also well known for its agricultural products. Although an ancient land, Italy only became a unified, independent country in 1870.

Find out all about Italy and Malta, and where in the world they are. Then look for all of the following things, too.

- Airplane
- Cook
- Cyclist
- Goat
- Gondola
- Horse
- Music note
- Octopus
- Paintbrush
- Pizza
- Prawn
- Roman soldiers (2)
- Sardines
- Scuba diver
- Skier
- Soccer ball
- Squid
- Stamp
- Swordfish

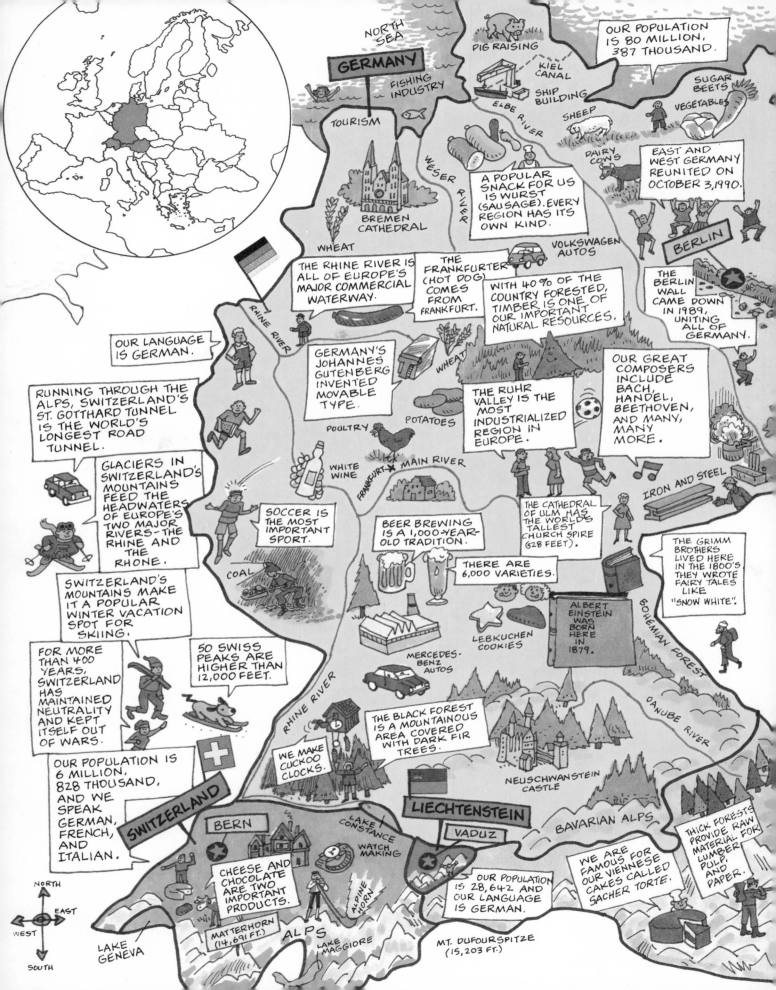

Central Europe

From north to south, this region's landscape changes from marshy plains to snowcapped mountains. It is crossed by two of Europe's longest rivers—the Rhine and the Danube—and by the famous Alps, the longest and highest mountain range in western Europe.

Find out all about the countries of central Europe, and where in the world they are. Then look for all of the following things, too.

- ☐ Automobiles (3)
- ☐ Axe
- ☐ Berlin Wall
- ☐ Books (3)
- ☐ Cake
- ☐ Chicken
- ☐ Coal miner
- ☐ Cookies
- ☐ Cows (2)
- ☐ Cuckoo clock
- ☐ Dogs (2)
- ☐ Heron
- ☐ Horse
- ☐ Hot dog
- ☐ Pigs (2)
- ☐ Soccer ball
- ☐ Telescope
- ☐ Tuba
- ☐ Watch

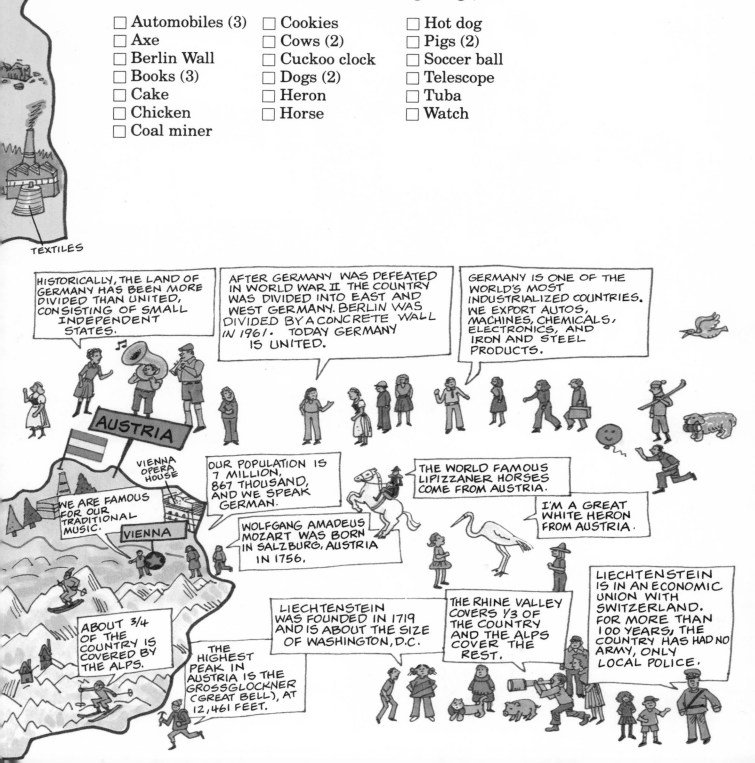

BALTIC SEA

TEXTILES

HISTORICALLY, THE LAND OF GERMANY HAS BEEN MORE DIVIDED THAN UNITED, CONSISTING OF SMALL INDEPENDENT STATES.

AFTER GERMANY WAS DEFEATED IN WORLD WAR II THE COUNTRY WAS DIVIDED INTO EAST AND WEST GERMANY. BERLIN WAS DIVIDED BY A CONCRETE WALL IN 1961. TODAY GERMANY IS UNITED.

GERMANY IS ONE OF THE WORLD'S MOST INDUSTRIALIZED COUNTRIES. WE EXPORT AUTOS, MACHINES, CHEMICALS, ELECTRONICS, AND IRON AND STEEL PRODUCTS.

AUSTRIA

VIENNA OPERA HOUSE

WE ARE FAMOUS FOR OUR TRADITIONAL MUSIC.

VIENNA

OUR POPULATION IS 7 MILLION, 867 THOUSAND, AND WE SPEAK GERMAN.

WOLFGANG AMADEUS MOZART WAS BORN IN SALZBURG, AUSTRIA IN 1756.

THE WORLD FAMOUS LIPIZZANER HORSES COME FROM AUSTRIA.

I'M A GREAT WHITE HERON FROM AUSTRIA.

ABOUT 3/4 OF THE COUNTRY IS COVERED BY THE ALPS.

THE HIGHEST PEAK IN AUSTRIA IS THE GROSSGLOCKNER (GREAT BELL), AT 12,461 FEET.

LIECHTENSTEIN WAS FOUNDED IN 1719 AND IS ABOUT THE SIZE OF WASHINGTON, D.C.

THE RHINE VALLEY COVERS 1/3 OF THE COUNTRY AND THE ALPS COVER THE REST.

LIECHTENSTEIN IS IN AN ECONOMIC UNION WITH SWITZERLAND. FOR MORE THAN 100 YEARS, THE COUNTRY HAS HAD NO ARMY, ONLY LOCAL POLICE.

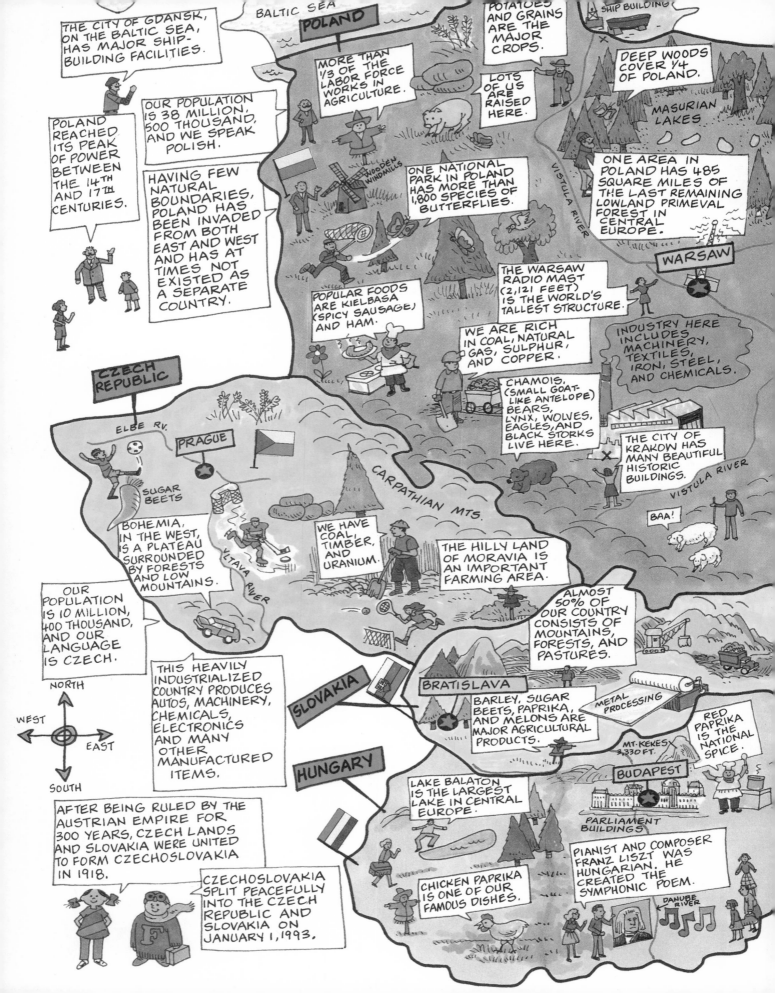

Eastern Europe

The boundaries and leadership of these central European countries has changed many times. Dominated by the Soviet Union since the end of World War II, they are now moving toward more democratic forms of government.

Find out all about the countries of Eastern Europe, and where in the world they are. Then look for all of the following things, too.

- ☐ Barn
- ☐ Bear
- ☐ Bird
- ☐ Bison
- ☐ Butterflies (4)
- ☐ Carrot
- ☐ Cooks (3)
- ☐ Flower
- ☐ Hockey player
- ☐ Music notes
- ☐ Pigs (2)
- ☐ Radio tower
- ☐ Sausage
- ☐ Scarecrows (5)
- ☐ Sheep
- ☐ Tennis ball
- ☐ Tourists
- ☐ Truck
- ☐ Windmill
- ☐ Woolly mammoth

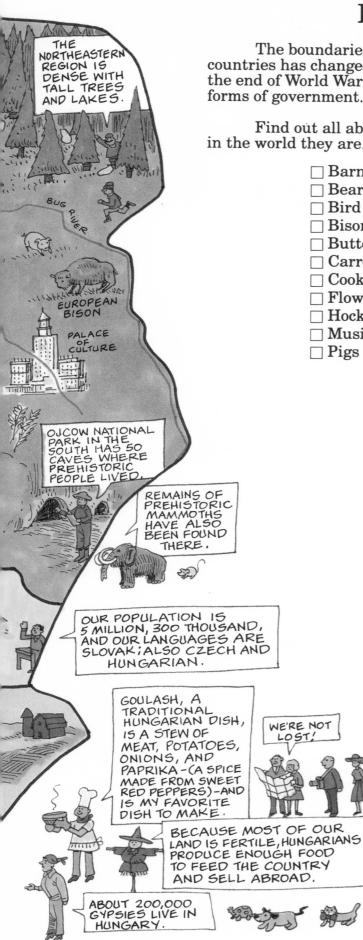

THE NORTHEASTERN REGION IS DENSE WITH TALL TREES AND LAKES.

BUG RIVER

EUROPEAN BISON

PALACE OF CULTURE

OJCOW NATIONAL PARK IN THE SOUTH HAS 50 CAVES WHERE PREHISTORIC PEOPLE LIVED.

REMAINS OF PREHISTORIC MAMMOTHS HAVE ALSO BEEN FOUND THERE.

OUR POPULATION IS 5 MILLION, 300 THOUSAND, AND OUR LANGUAGES ARE SLOVAK; ALSO CZECH AND HUNGARIAN.

GOULASH, A TRADITIONAL HUNGARIAN DISH, IS A STEW OF MEAT, POTATOES, ONIONS, AND PAPRIKA—(A SPICE MADE FROM SWEET RED PEPPERS)—AND IS MY FAVORITE DISH TO MAKE.

WE'RE NOT LOST!

BECAUSE MOST OF OUR LAND IS FERTILE, HUNGARIANS PRODUCE ENOUGH FOOD TO FEED THE COUNTRY AND SELL ABROAD.

ABOUT 200,000 GYPSIES LIVE IN HUNGARY.

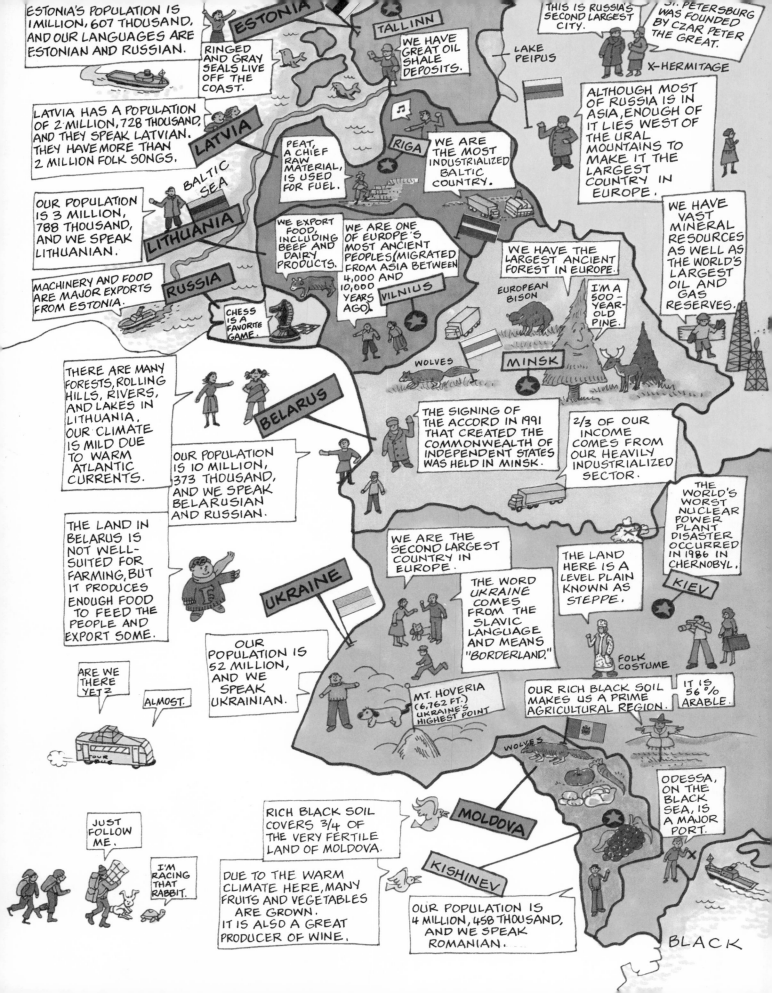

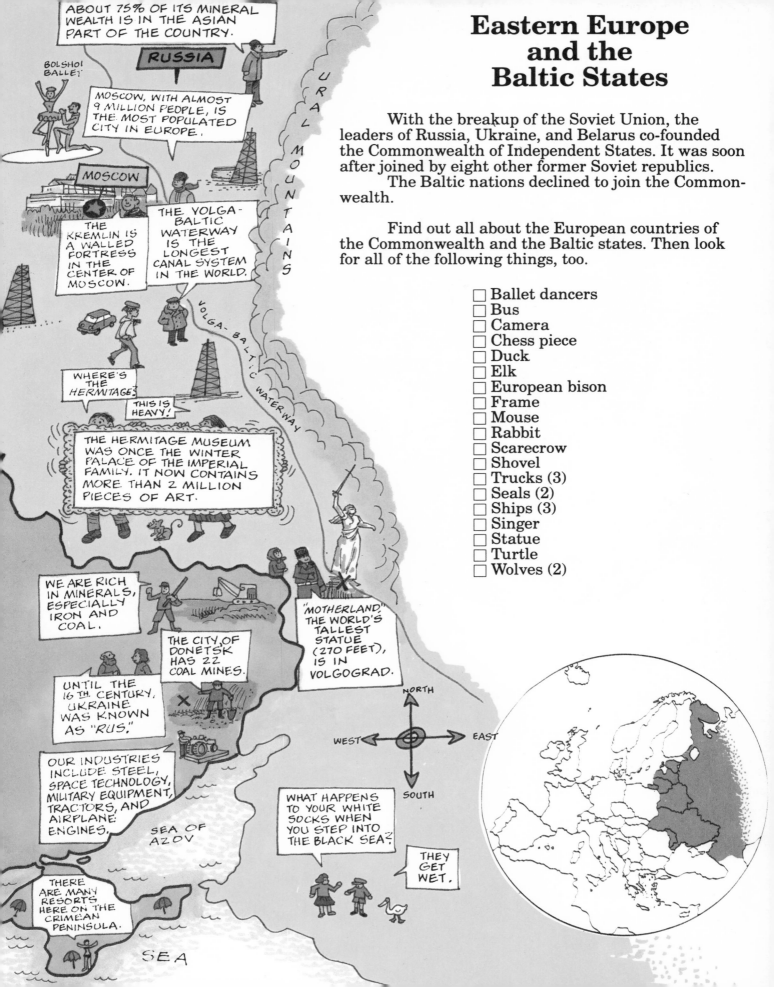

Eastern Europe and the Baltic States

With the breakup of the Soviet Union, the leaders of Russia, Ukraine, and Belarus co-founded the Commonwealth of Independent States. It was soon after joined by eight other former Soviet republics.

The Baltic nations declined to join the Commonwealth.

Find out all about the European countries of the Commonwealth and the Baltic states. Then look for all of the following things, too.

- ☐ Ballet dancers
- ☐ Bus
- ☐ Camera
- ☐ Chess piece
- ☐ Duck
- ☐ Elk
- ☐ European bison
- ☐ Frame
- ☐ Mouse
- ☐ Rabbit
- ☐ Scarecrow
- ☐ Shovel
- ☐ Trucks (3)
- ☐ Seals (2)
- ☐ Ships (3)
- ☐ Singer
- ☐ Statue
- ☐ Turtle
- ☐ Wolves (2)

The Balkan States

Much of the land known as the Balkan states was ruled by Turkey from the end of the 15th century until 1913. After the end of World War I, the Balkan country of Yugoslavia was created when several regions were combined into a federation of six republics. Divided by nationalistic and religious differences, the republics began to separate into independent nations in 1991. Former Yugoslavia consists of Serbia and Montenegro, Slovenia, Croatia, Bosnia and Herzegovina, and Macedonia.

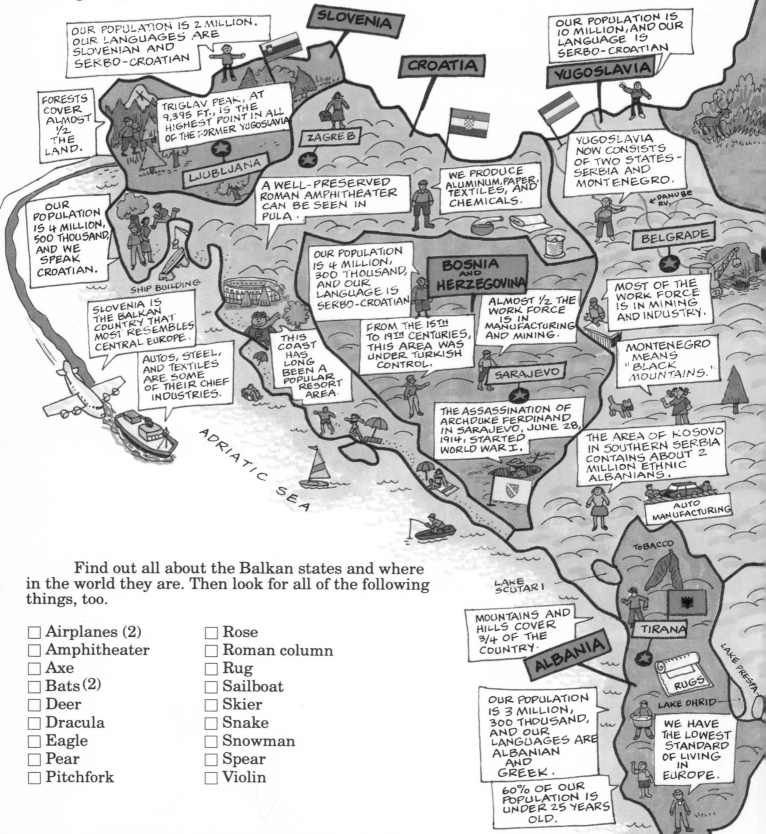

Find out all about the Balkan states and where in the world they are. Then look for all of the following things, too.

- ☐ Airplanes (2)
- ☐ Amphitheater
- ☐ Axe
- ☐ Bats (2)
- ☐ Deer
- ☐ Dracula
- ☐ Eagle
- ☐ Pear
- ☐ Pitchfork
- ☐ Rose
- ☐ Roman column
- ☐ Rug
- ☐ Sailboat
- ☐ Skier
- ☐ Snake
- ☐ Snowman
- ☐ Spear
- ☐ Violin

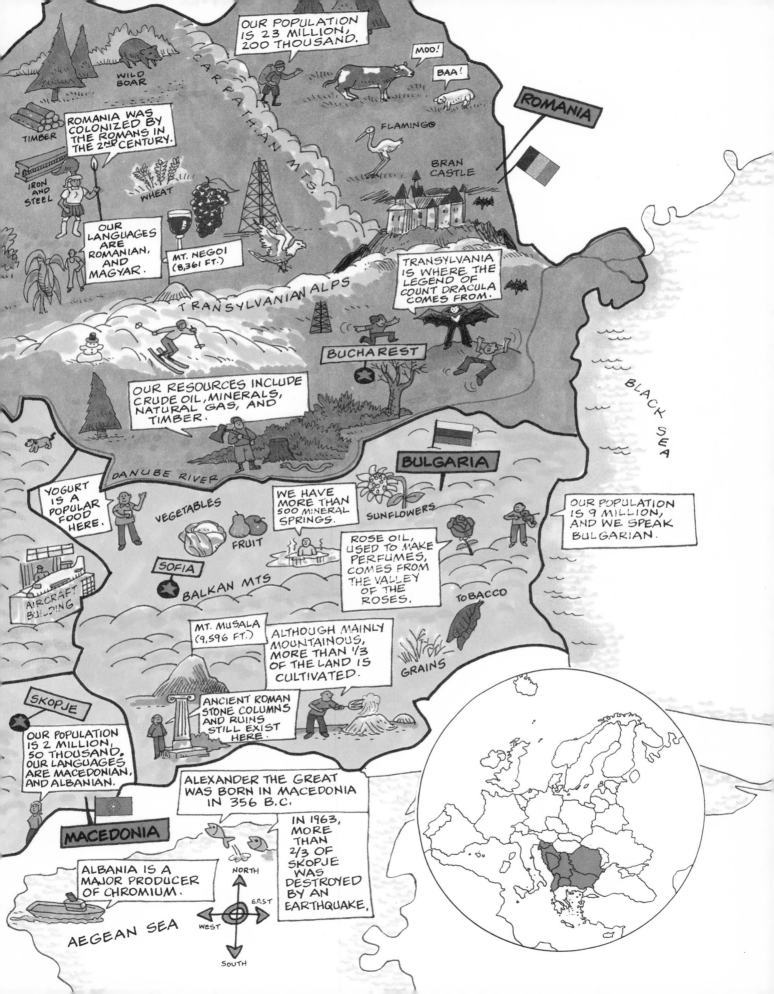

Greece

The ideals of western democracy were born in Greece about 2,500 years ago. The art, philosophy, theater, mythology, science, and architecture that flourished there formed the basis of western civilization.

Find out all about Greece and where in the world it is. Then look for all of the following things, too.

☐ Book ☐ Dolphin ☐ Olympic torch bearer
☐ Camera ☐ Grapes ☐ Sailboat
☐ Cotton ☐ Octopus ☐ Vase

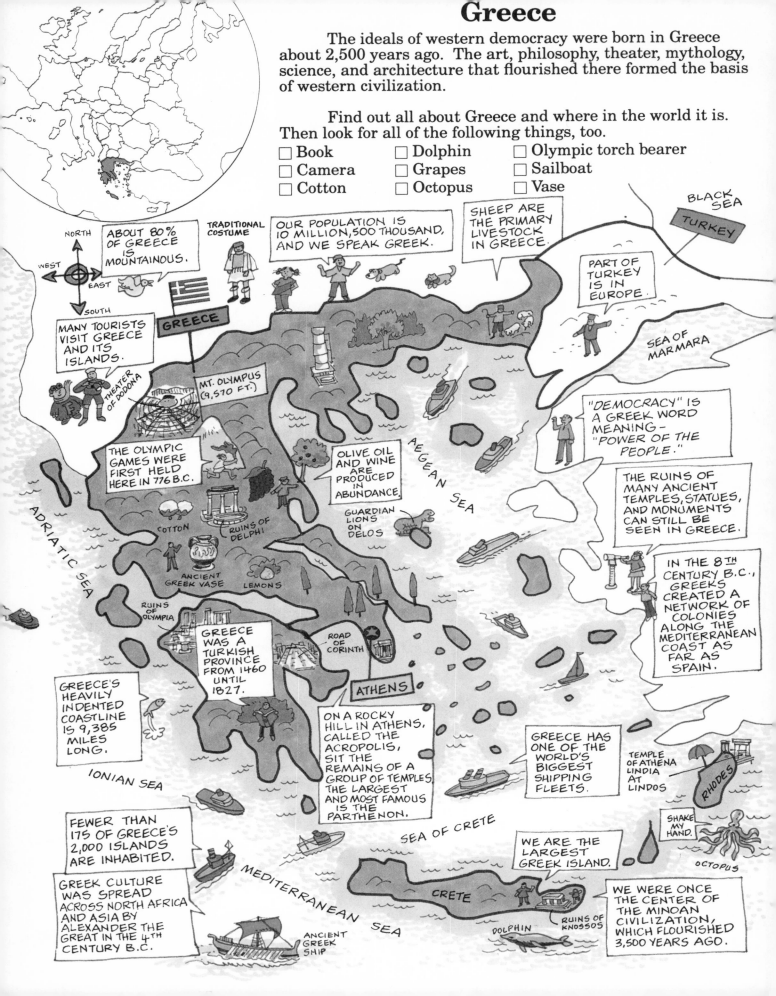

WHERE IN THE WORLD ARE WE NOW?

AFRICA

By
Anthony Tallarico

Copyright © 1994 Kidsbooks, Inc. and Anthony Tallarico
3535 West Peterson Avenue
Chicago, IL 60659

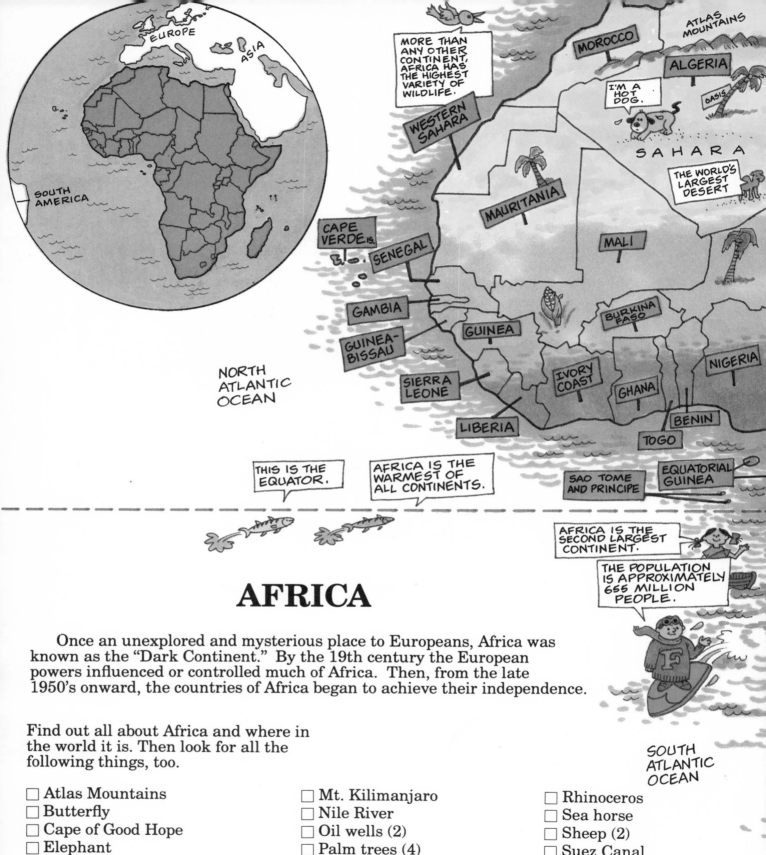

AFRICA

Once an unexplored and mysterious place to Europeans, Africa was known as the "Dark Continent." By the 19th century the European powers influenced or controlled much of Africa. Then, from the late 1950's onward, the countries of Africa began to achieve their independence.

Find out all about Africa and where in the world it is. Then look for all the following things, too.

☐ Atlas Mountains
☐ Butterfly
☐ Cape of Good Hope
☐ Elephant
☐ Gold bar
☐ Indian Ocean

☐ Mt. Kilimanjaro
☐ Nile River
☐ Oil wells (2)
☐ Palm trees (4)
☐ Pyramid
☐ Rain cloud

☐ Rhinoceros
☐ Sea horse
☐ Sheep (2)
☐ Suez Canal
☐ Umbrella
☐ Zebra

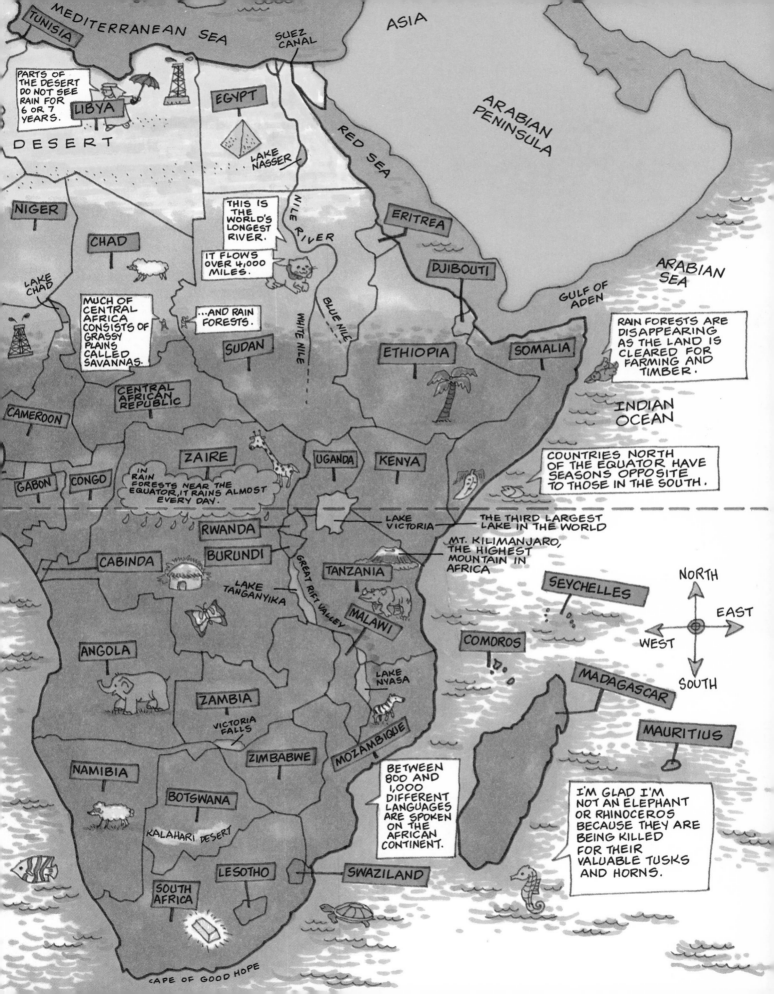

NORTH AFRICA

North of the Sahara, ancient Egyptians, Greeks, Romans, and peoples of Arabia have influenced African cultures. Today, in North Africa, the Arabic language is dominant and the major religion is Islam.

Find out all about North Africa
and where in the world it is. Then
look for all the following things, too.

☐ Barbary ape
☐ Beret
☐ Boats (3)
☐ Bunch of grapes
☐ Hyena

☐ Miner
☐ Orange tree
☐ Oil wells (4)
☐ Ostrich

☐ Pencil
☐ Pirate
☐ Pyramids (4)
☐ Scarecrow

☐ Scorpion
☐ Shovel
☐ Snake
☐ Thermometer

THE SAHEL

Below the deserts of North Africa is the Sahel, a region long inhabited by animal grazers and farmers. As the Sahara expands south — about 3 miles each year — much of the Sahel is becoming part of the desert.

Find out all about the Sahel and where in the world it is. Then look for all the following things, too.

- ☐ Anchor
- ☐ Basket
- ☐ Bird
- ☐ Camels (5)
- ☐ Cotton balls (3)
- ☐ Goat
- ☐ Elephant
- ☐ Fisherman
- ☐ Hippopotamus
- ☐ Lake Chad
- ☐ Niger River
- ☐ Peanuts (3)
- ☐ Periscope
- ☐ Soccer ball
- ☐ Sun
- ☐ Tent

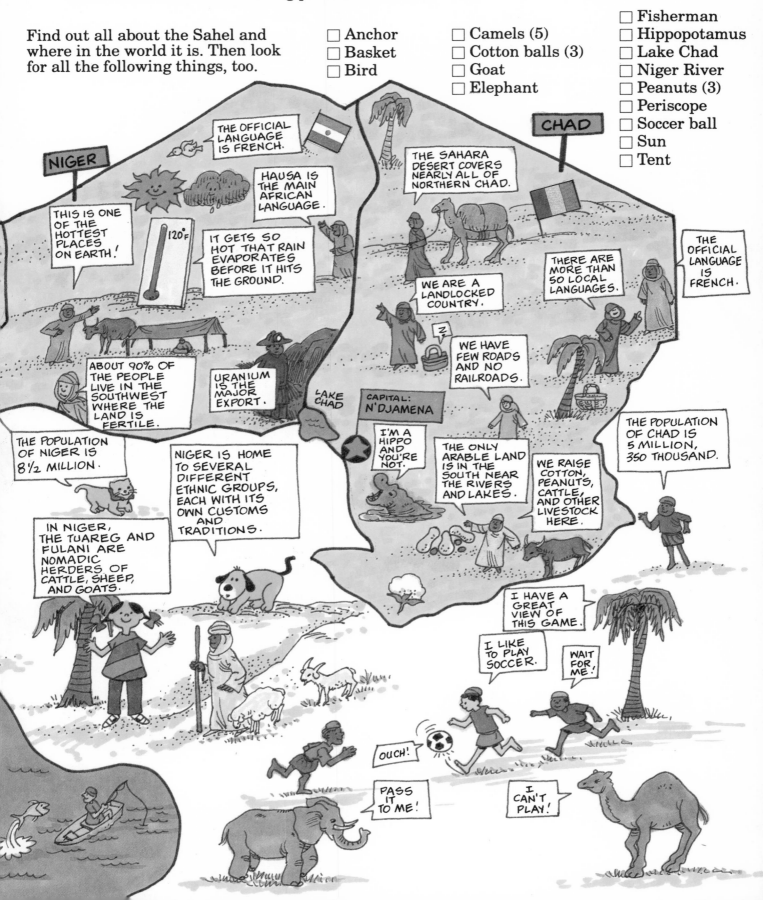

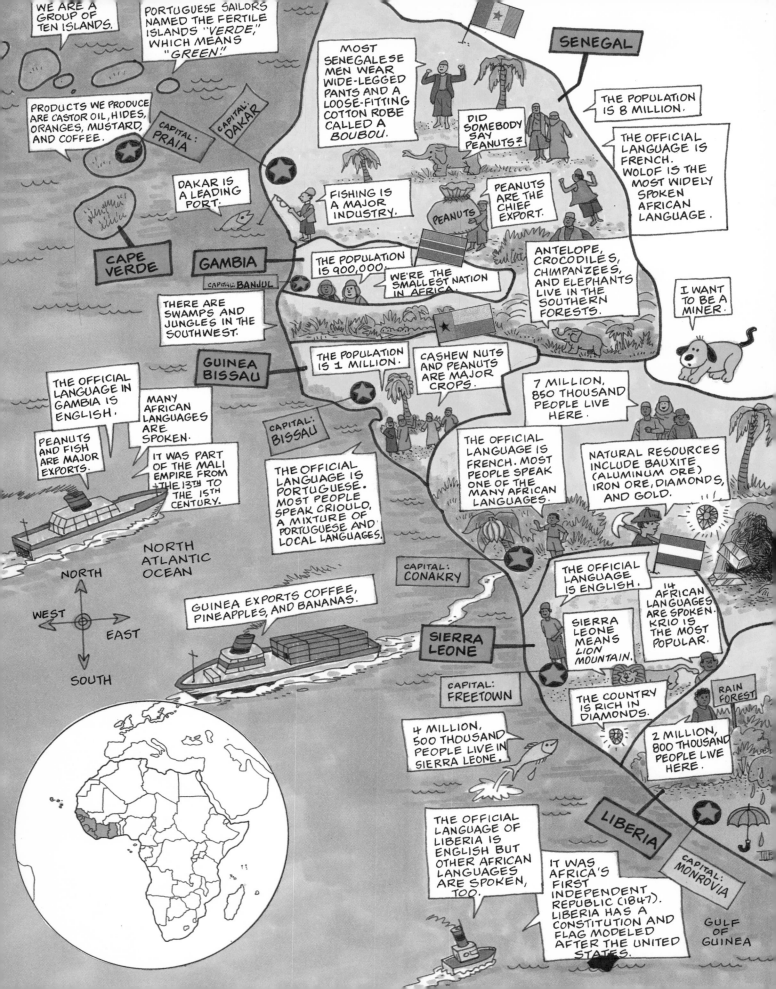

THE WESTERN COAST

The landscape of the western coast of Africa varies from humid coastal plains and swamps to forested hills and plateaus. The soil is fertile, and crops such as cocoa, coffee, and peanuts are grown.

During the era of the slave trade to the Americas, and for centuries before with other nations, coastal kingdoms of West Africa grew rich by trading slaves, gold, and ivory.

Find out all about the western coast of Africa and where in the world it is. Then look for all the following things, too.

- ☐ Boats (4)
- ☐ Chocolate bar
- ☐ Coffeepot
- ☐ Crocodile
- ☐ Diamonds (4)
- ☐ Elephants (4)
- ☐ Fisherman
- ☐ Game warden
- ☐ Gold bars (3)
- ☐ Lake Volta
- ☐ Lion
- ☐ Miner
- ☐ Pygmy hippopotamus
- ☐ Rain clouds (2)
- ☐ Umbrella

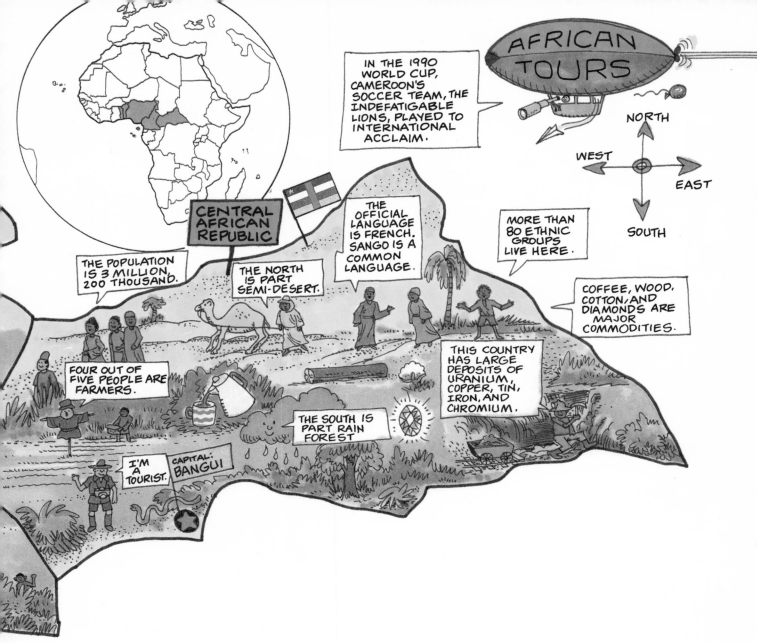

CENTRAL AFRICA

The countries on the Gulf of Guinea share part of the old "slave coast." Their landscape is incredibly varied, with old volcanic mountains, semi-desert regions, savannas, swamps, and tropical rain forests.

Find out all about the countries of central Africa and where in the world they are. Then look for all the following things, too.

- ☐ Camera
- ☐ Cup
- ☐ Fishing poles (2)
- ☐ Giraffe
- ☐ Huts (2)
- ☐ Life preserver
- ☐ Oil wells (3)
- ☐ Paper airplane
- ☐ Red car
- ☐ Scarecrow
- ☐ Shark
- ☐ Snakes (2)
- ☐ Telescope
- ☐ Umbrellas (2)
- ☐ Volcano

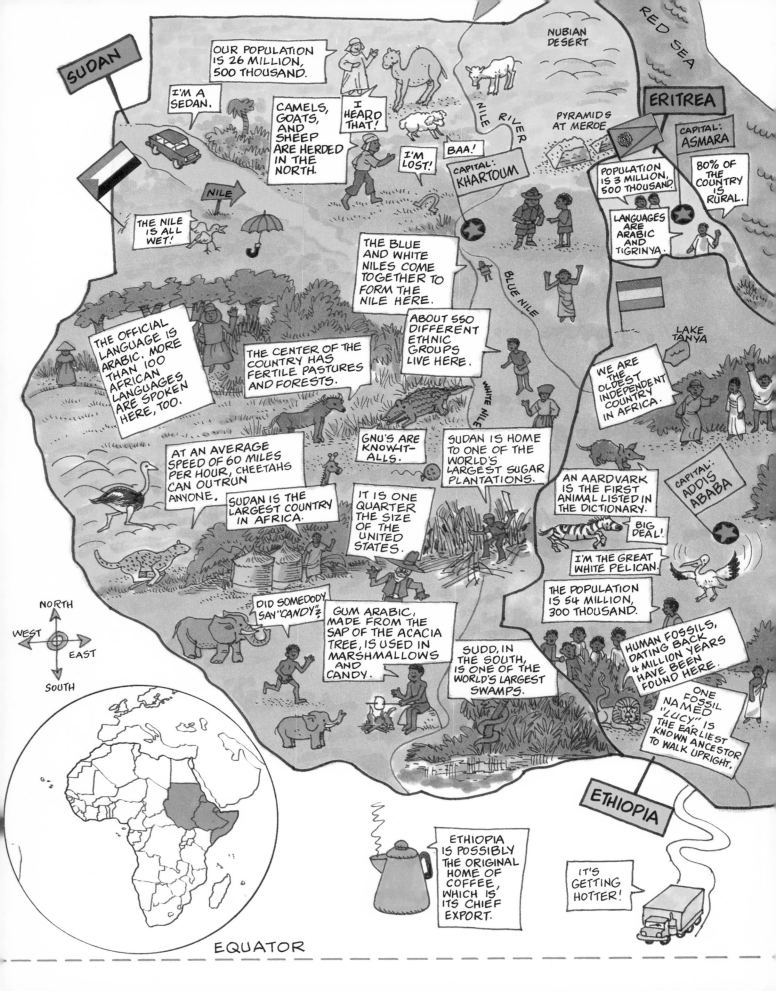

THE HORN OF AFRICA

The region on the eastern coast is known as the Horn of Africa. On the map, it looks like the horn of a rhinoceros jutting into the Indian Ocean.

Find out all about the Horn of Africa and where in the world it is. Then look for all the following things, too.

- ☐ Aardvark
- ☐ Acacia tree
- ☐ Banana
- ☐ Coffeepot
- ☐ Cotton
- ☐ Giraffes (2)
- ☐ Horseshoe
- ☐ Lion
- ☐ Marshmallow
- ☐ Nile crocodile
- ☐ Nubian Desert
- ☐ Oryx
- ☐ Ostrich
- ☐ Red Sea
- ☐ Umbrella
- ☐ White Nile
- ☐ Zebra

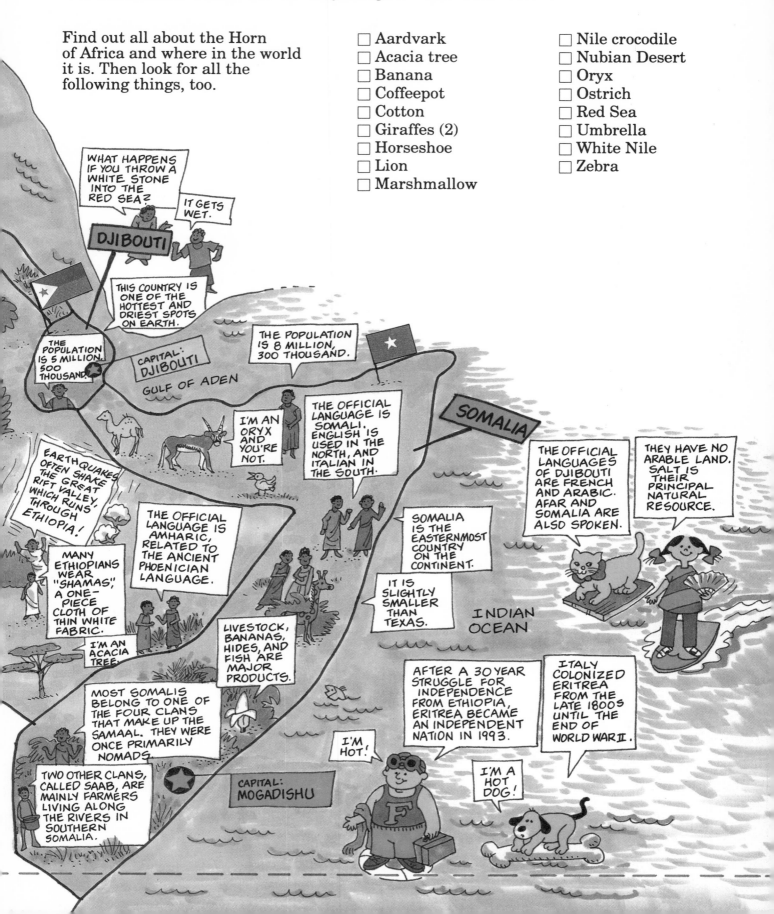

I'M A TUNA... ARE YOU?

GABON'S POPULATION IS 1 MILLION, 100 THOUSAND.

THE POPULATION IS 400 THOUSAND.

CAPITAL: MALABO

THIS COUNTRY IS MADE UP OF A MAINLAND, CALLED RIO MUNI, AND 5 ISLANDS.

GABON

CONGO

WE'RE COVERED BY DENSE FORESTS

WE ARE THE ONLY AFRICAN COUNTRY WITH SPANISH AS THE OFFICIAL LANGUAGE.

EQUATORIAL GUINEA

OUR POPULATION IS 2 MILLION 400 THOUSAND.

FANG IS THE NATIVE TONGUE.

WE ARE HOME TO MORE THAN 3,000 SPECIES OF VEGETATION.

THE OFFICIAL LANGUAGE IS FRENCH. FANG, MBERE, AND SIRA PUNU ARE SOME OF THE LOCAL LANGUAGES.

THE SLAVE TRADE FLOURISHED HERE FOR FOUR CENTURIES.

NORTH
WEST
EAST
SOUTH

CAPITAL: LIBREVILLE

EQUATOR

EQUATORIAL AFRICA

WE ARE RICH IN NATURAL RESOURCES SUCH AS MANGANESE, URANIUM, OIL, AND IRON.

ALLEN'S SWAMP MONKEYS, NOW ENDANGERED, LIVE NEAR THE WATER.

Located on or near the equator, much of the land in these countries is covered with tropical forests.

THE OFFICIAL LANGUAGE IS FRENCH. THE MAIN AFRICAN LANGUAGES ARE LINGALA AND MUNUKUTUBA.

CAPITAL: BRAZZAVILLE

Find out all about equatorial Africa and where in the world it is. Then look for all the following things, too.

I'M AN OIL PALM.

CAPITAL: KINSHASA

□ Buffalo
□ Congo River
□ Crocodile
□ Cup
□ Diamonds (3)
□ Elephants (3)
□ Envelope
□ Flashlight
□ Lake Tanganyika
□ Miners (2)
□ Monkeys with tails (2)
□ Snakes (2)
□ Shovel
□ Tires (2)
□ Truck
□ Umbrella

SOUTH ATLANTIC OCEAN

SUGAR CANE IS EXPORTED FROM THE CONGO.

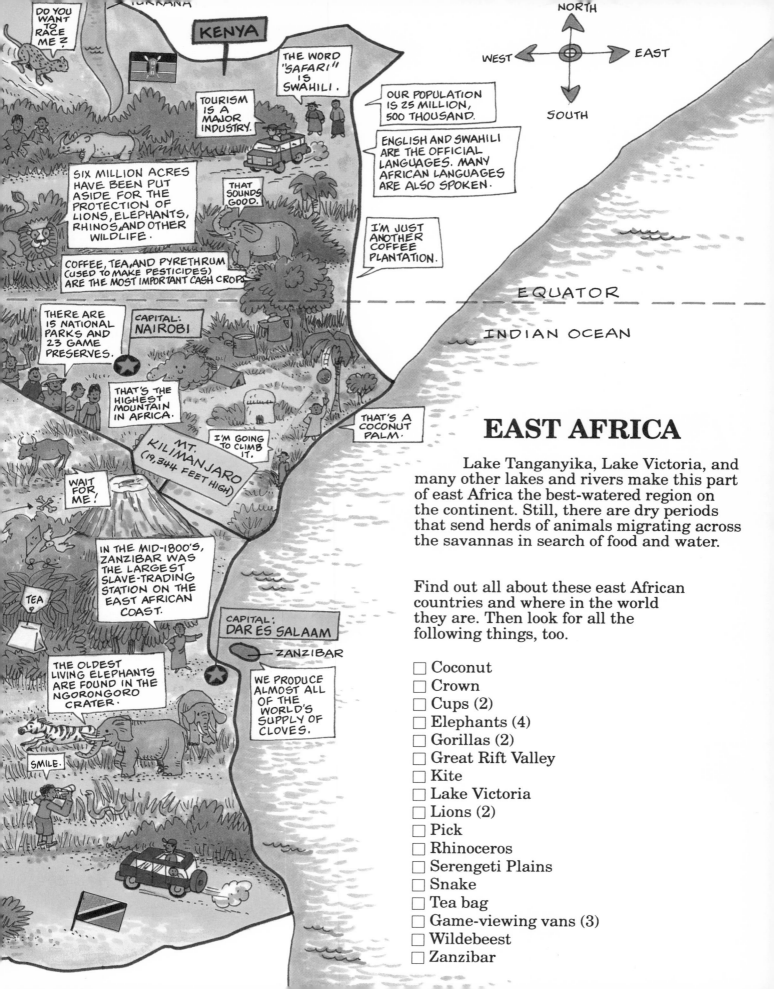

EAST AFRICA

Lake Tanganyika, Lake Victoria, and many other lakes and rivers make this part of east Africa the best-watered region on the continent. Still, there are dry periods that send herds of animals migrating across the savannas in search of food and water.

Find out all about these east African countries and where in the world they are. Then look for all the following things, too.

- ☐ Coconut
- ☐ Crown
- ☐ Cups (2)
- ☐ Elephants (4)
- ☐ Gorillas (2)
- ☐ Great Rift Valley
- ☐ Kite
- ☐ Lake Victoria
- ☐ Lions (2)
- ☐ Pick
- ☐ Rhinoceros
- ☐ Serengeti Plains
- ☐ Snake
- ☐ Tea bag
- ☐ Game-viewing vans (3)
- ☐ Wildebeest
- ☐ Zanzibar

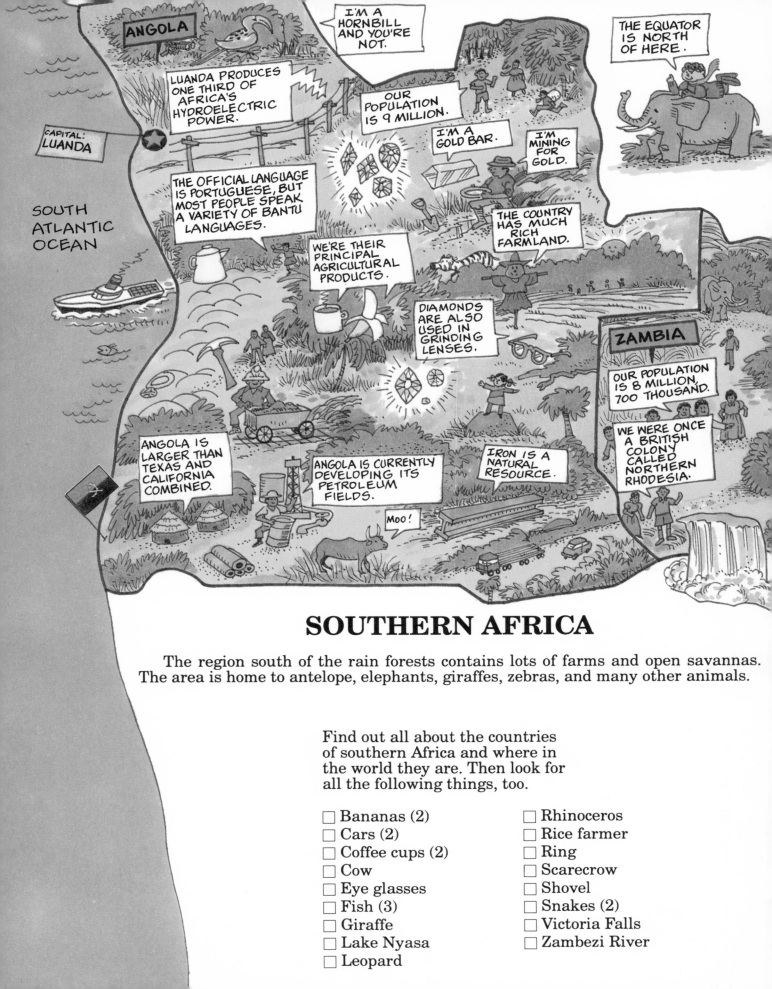

SOUTHERN AFRICA

The region south of the rain forests contains lots of farms and open savannas. The area is home to antelope, elephants, giraffes, zebras, and many other animals.

Find out all about the countries of southern Africa and where in the world they are. Then look for all the following things, too.

- ☐ Bananas (2)
- ☐ Cars (2)
- ☐ Coffee cups (2)
- ☐ Cow
- ☐ Eye glasses
- ☐ Fish (3)
- ☐ Giraffe
- ☐ Lake Nyasa
- ☐ Leopard
- ☐ Rhinoceros
- ☐ Rice farmer
- ☐ Ring
- ☐ Scarecrow
- ☐ Shovel
- ☐ Snakes (2)
- ☐ Victoria Falls
- ☐ Zambezi River

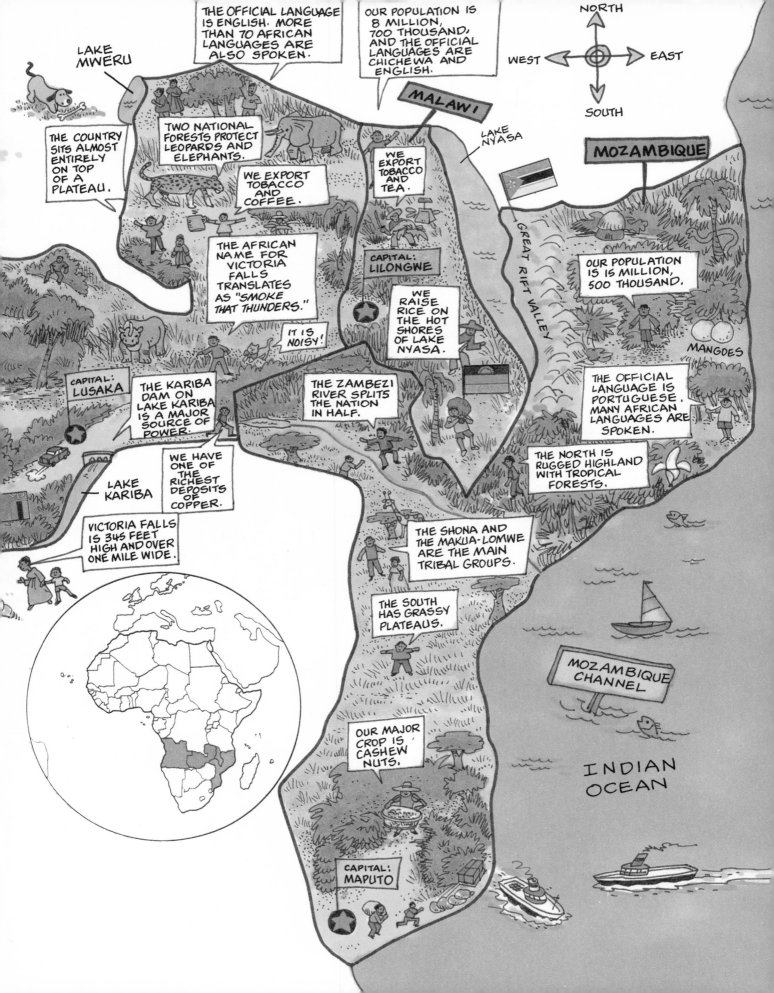

...SOUTHERN AFRICA

Rich deposits of diamonds, gold, and minerals make this area one of the fastest-growing economic regions in Africa.

Find out more about the countries of southern Africa and where in the world they are. Then look for all the following things, too.

- ☐ Baby
- ☐ Billboard
- ☐ Book
- ☐ Elephants (6)
- ☐ Fishing pole
- ☐ Lions (2)
- ☐ Lost snowman
- ☐ Namib Desert
- ☐ Oryx
- ☐ Picks (2)
- ☐ Rake
- ☐ Scorpion
- ☐ Shipwreck
- ☐ Snakes (5)
- ☐ Sneaker
- ☐ Truck
- ☐ Zebras (2)

THE CAPE OF AFRICA

The world's greatest diamond and gold mines are in South Africa, making it the richest country in Africa. The mines employ tens of thousands of men from neighboring countries.

Find out all about the cape of Africa and where in the world it is. Then look for all the following things, too.

- ☐ Cars (4)
- ☐ Citrus fruit
- ☐ Crown
- ☐ Drummer
- ☐ Giraffes (3)
- ☐ Grapes
- ☐ Guitar
- ☐ Lion
- ☐ Orange River
- ☐ Ostrich
- ☐ Pineapple
- ☐ Sailor
- ☐ Scarecrow
- ☐ Sheep (2)
- ☐ Shovel
- ☐ Table Mountain
- ☐ Tent
- ☐ Tractor
- ☐ Zebra
- ☐ Zulu warrior

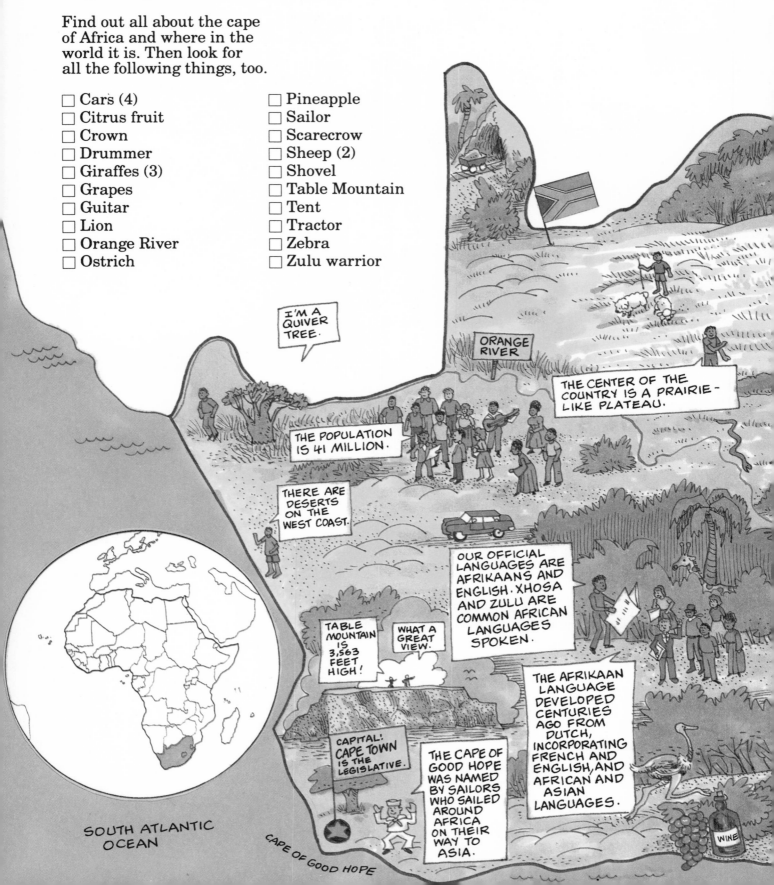

THE ISLAND NATIONS

Many of the tropical islands off the southeast coast of Africa in the Indian Ocean are volcanic in origin.

ABOUT HALF OF THE ISLANDS ARE MADE OF CORAL, AND MOST ARE UNINHABITED.

POPULATION IS 70,000!

FOR RENT

CAPITAL: MORONI

COMOROS

THE OFFICIAL LANGUAGES ARE ARABIC AND FRENCH, BUT MOST PEOPLE SPEAK COMORAN (A FORM OF SWAHILI).

THE POPULATION IS 500 THOUSAND.

THE NATION IS MADE UP OF THREE VOLCANIC ISLANDS.

PERFUME OILS ARE A KEY EXPORT.

SEYCHELLES

THE NATION IS MADE UP OF 90 SCATTERED ISLANDS.

CAPITAL: VICTORIA

THE OFFICIAL LANGUAGES ARE ENGLISH AND FRENCH, BUT MOST PEOPLE SPEAK CREOLE.

VACANCY

INDIAN OCEAN

MADAGASCAR

Find out all about the island nations off the coast of Africa and where in the world they are. Then look for all the following things, too.

- ☐ Anchor
- ☐ Butterflies (3)
- ☐ Coffeepot
- ☐ Fish (3)
- ☐ Lemurs (2)
- ☐ Perfume bottle
- ☐ Periscope
- ☐ Tortoise

WE'RE THE WORLD'S FOURTH LARGEST ISLAND.

WE'RE VANILLA PODS.

MANY SPECIES OF OUR ANIMALS ARE IN DANGER OF EXTINCTION.

THE POPULATION OF MAURITIUS IS 1 MILLION, 121 THOUSAND.

THE OFFICIAL LANGUAGES ARE ENGLISH AND FRENCH.

MOST OF THE PEOPLE SPEAK CREOLE.

WE'RE ABOUT THE SIZE OF RHODE ISLAND.

THAT'S A PLOWSHARE TORTOISE.

THE RAIN FORESTS ARE DISAPPEARING DUE TO FARMING AND EROSION.

OUR POPULATION IS 12 MILLION, 500 THOUSAND.

THE EAST COAST IS HUMID AND DENSELY POPULATED.

ABOUT 20 DIFFERENT KINDS OF LEMUR CAN BE FOUND ONLY HERE.

ALL FOUR ISLANDS ARE VOLCANIC IN ORIGIN.

THE EXTINCT DODO BIRD LIVED HERE.

WE'RE ABOUT THE SIZE OF TEXAS.

SCIENTISTS BELIEVE THIS ISLAND BROKE AWAY FROM MAINLAND AFRICA OVER 160 MILLION YEARS AGO.

BAOBAB TREE

THE OFFICIAL LANGUAGES ARE FRENCH AND MALAGASY.

CAPITAL: ANTANANARIVO

N.
W.
E.
S.

MOST ISLANDERS TRACE THEIR ANCESTRY TO INDIA.

WE WERE SETTLED BY MALAYAN-INDONESIAN PEOPLE 2,000 YEARS AGO.

COFFEE IS THE NUMBER ONE CASH CROP.

MAURITIUS

CAPITAL: PORT LOUIS

THIS ISLAND HAS 1,000 TYPES OF ORCHIDS AND 200 SPECIES OF BUTTERFLIES.

SHAKE HANDS! I'M AN OCTOPUS TREE.

DUE TO ITS ISOLATION, MANY ANIMALS AND PLANTS CAN ONLY BE FOUND IN MADAGASCAR.

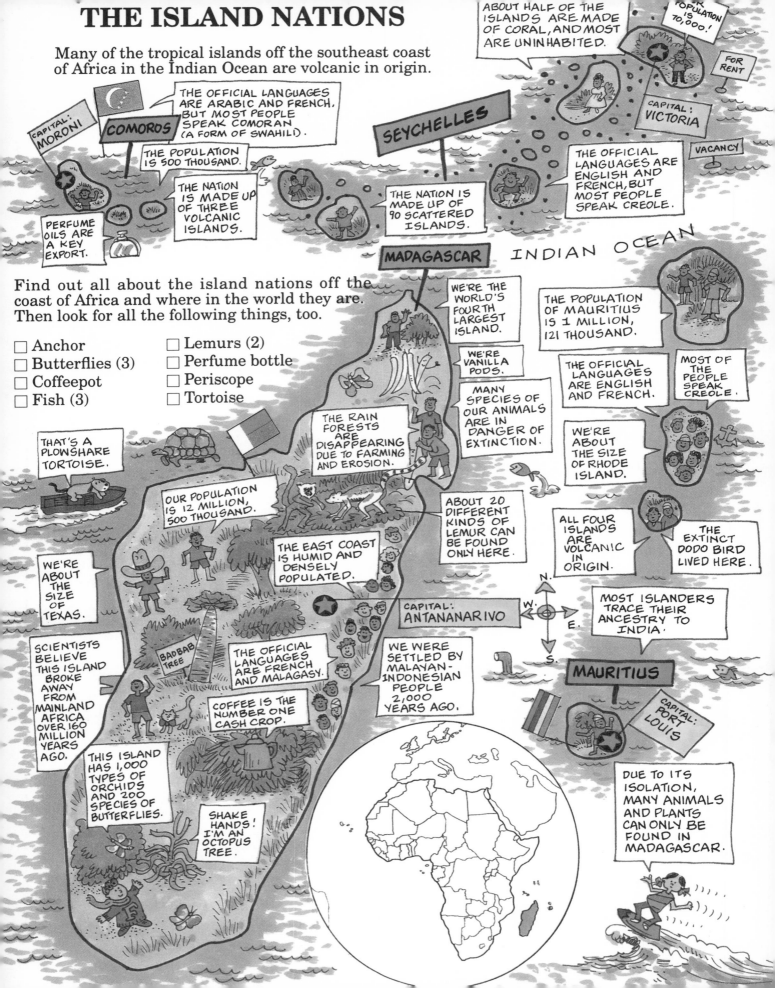

WHERE IN THE WORLD ARE WE NOW ?

NORTH and SOUTH AMERICA

By
Anthony Tallarico

Copyright © 1994 Kidsbooks, Inc. and Anthony Tallarico
3535 West Peterson Avenue
Chicago, IL 60659

Manufactured in the United States of America

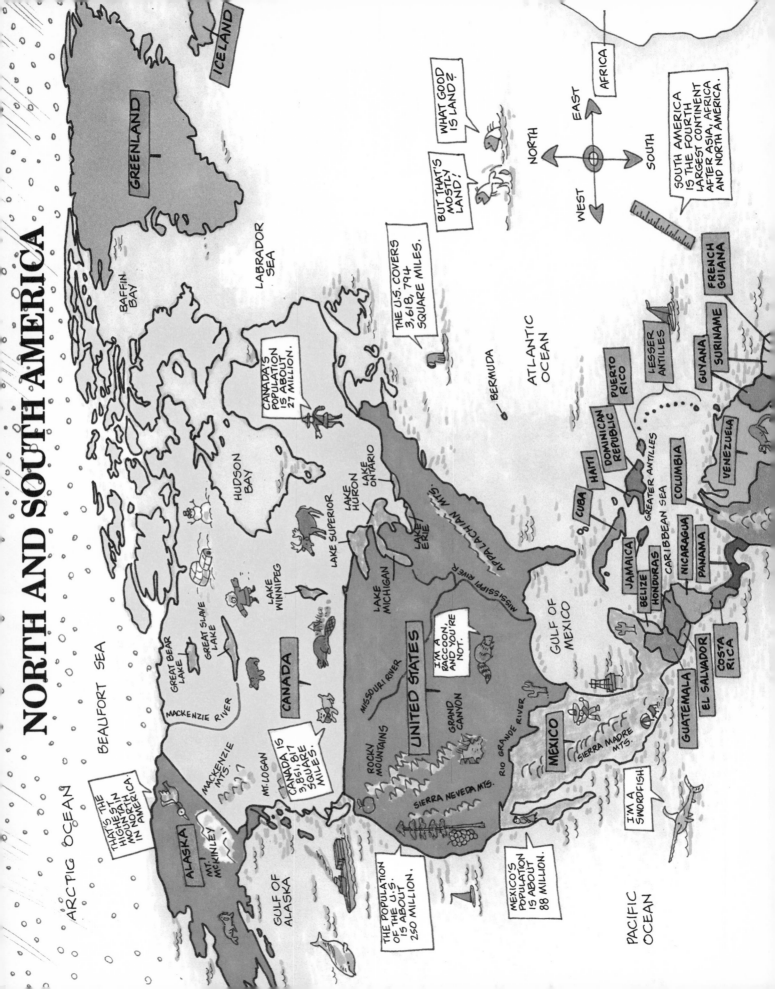

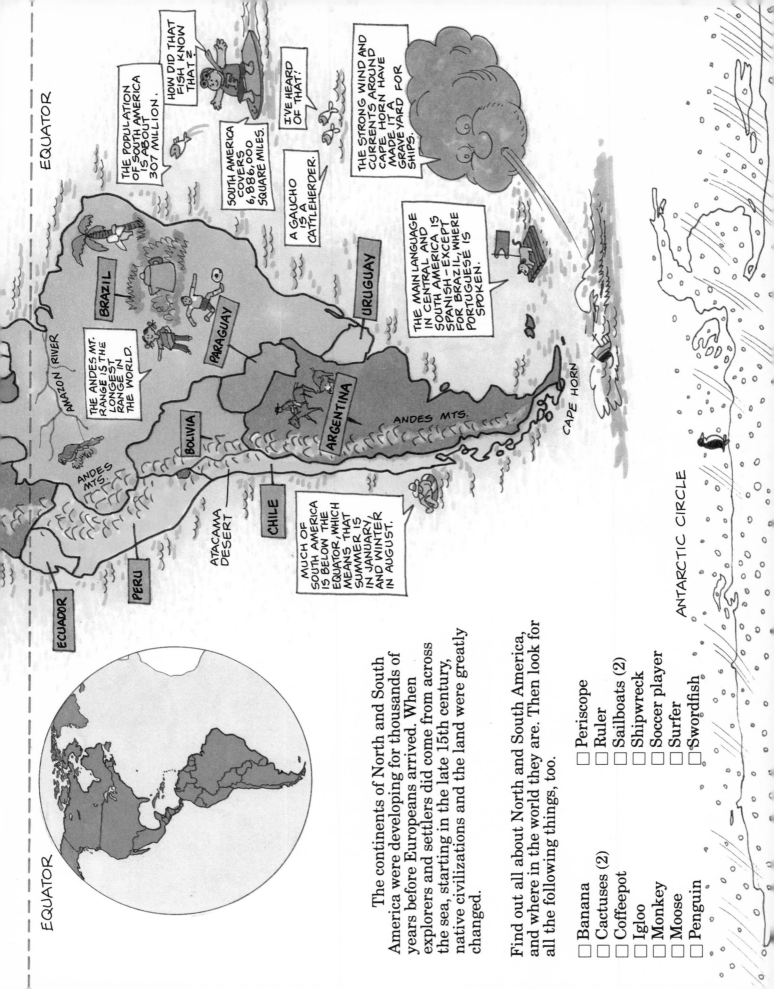

EQUATOR

THE POPULATION OF SOUTH AMERICA IS ABOUT 307 MILLION.

HOW DID THAT FISH KNOW THAT?

SOUTH AMERICA COVERS 6,886,000 SQUARE MILES.

I'VE HEARD OF THAT!

A GAUCHO IS A CATTLEHERDER.

THE STRONG WIND AND CURRENTS AROUND CAPE HORN HAVE MADE IT A GRAVEYARD FOR SHIPS.

BRAZIL

URUGUAY

PARAGUAY

THE MAIN LANGUAGE IN CENTRAL AND SOUTH AMERICA IS SPANISH—EXCEPT FOR BRAZIL, WHERE PORTUGUESE IS SPOKEN.

AMAZON RIVER

THE ANDES MT. RANGE IS THE LONGEST RANGE IN THE WORLD.

ARGENTINA

ANDES MTS.

BOLIVIA

ANDES MTS.

CAPE HORN

PERU

ATACAMA DESERT

CHILE

MUCH OF SOUTH AMERICA IS BELOW THE EQUATOR, WHICH MEANS THAT SUMMER IS IN JANUARY, AND WINTER IN AUGUST.

ECUADOR

ANTARCTIC CIRCLE

EQUATOR

The continents of North and South America were developing for thousands of years before Europeans arrived. When explorers and settlers did come from across the sea, starting in the late 15th century, native civilizations and the land were greatly changed.

Find out all about North and South America, and where in the world they are. Then look for all the following things, too.

☐ Banana
☐ Cactuses (2)
☐ Coffeepot
☐ Igloo
☐ Monkey
☐ Moose
☐ Penguin
☐ Periscope
☐ Ruler
☐ Sailboats (2)
☐ Shipwreck
☐ Soccer player
☐ Surfer
☐ Swordfish

CENTRAL AMERICA POPULATION/LANGUAGE

GUATEMALA	9,700,000	SPANISH
BELIZE	200,000	ENGLISH
EL SALVADOR	5,600,000	SPANISH
HONDURAS	5,500,000	SPANISH
NICARAGUA	4,100,000	SPANISH
COSTA RICA	3,200,000	SPANISH
PANAMA	2,400,000	SPANISH

MEXICO HAS THE LARGEST SPANISH-SPEAKING POPULATION OF ANY COUNTRY IN THE WORLD.

THE POPULATION IS 88 MILLION.

SINCE MUCH OF MEXICO IS DRY OR MOUNTAINOUS, WATER IS SCARCE.

THE SIERRA MADRE MOUNTAIN RANGES EXTEND FOR ABOUT 1500 MILES ALONG THE EAST AND WEST.

BAJA CALIFORNIA

GULF OF CALIFORNIA

PACIFIC OCEAN

RICE

WE'RE RICH IN MINERALS AND PRECIOUS METALS.

BEANS

SHRIMPS 'R US!

ABOUT 1/3 OF THE MEXICAN PEOPLE DESCENDED FROM THE AZTEC INDIANS.

COTTON, SHRIMP, COFFEE, FRUIT, AND VEGETABLES ARE MAJOR EXPORTS.

MEXICO

SQUASH

CORN

ABOUT 20 MILLION PEOPLE LIVE IN AND AROUND MEXICO CITY.

MEXICO CITY

WE'RE ONE OF THE LARGEST CITIES IN THE WORLD.

OLMEC HEAD

POPOCATEPETL VOLCANO 17,887 FEET

ACAPULCO

RIO GRANDE

UNITED STATES

WE EXPORT OIL.

GULF OF MEXICO

THE AZTEC INDIANS BUILT THEIR CAPITAL, TEOTIHUACAN (TAY-O-TEE-WA-CAN) IN THIS SAME AREA.

IT MEANS "THE CITY OF THE GODS."

WE'RE THE WORLD LEADER IN SILVER PRODUCTION.

MAYA CITY

BELIZE

BELIZE CITY

GUATEMALA

TOURISTS COME TO ACAPULCO, CANCUN, AND PUERTO VALLARTA.

GUATEMALA CITY

MAJOR MAYAN RUINS ARE IN THE NORTH.

SAN SALVADOR

EL SALVADOR

THIS IS THE MOST DENSELY POPULATED COUNTRY IN CENTRAL AMERICA.

MEXICO AND CENTRAL AMERICA

The peoples of both Mexico and Central America are mostly of Spanish or Indian ancestry, or a mixture of both. Mexico, a hot and dry region of North America, is rich in precious metals and petroleum. The seven countries of Central America are mainly agricultural. Dotted with active volcanoes, the land has jungles and high mountains, and the climate is hot and steamy, perfect for growing coffee, bananas, and other tropical crops.

Find out all about Mexico, Central America, and the Caribbean Islands, and where in the world they are. Then look for all the following things, too.

- ☐ Armadillo
- ☐ Coffeepots (3)
- ☐ Cotton (3)
- ☐ Diver
- ☐ Miner
- ☐ Oil well
- ☐ Photographer
- ☐ Pineapple
- ☐ Sailor
- ☐ Scarecrow
- ☐ Shovel
- ☐ Shrimp (3)
- ☐ Squash
- ☐ Turtle
- ☐ Umbrellas (3)

THE CARIBBEAN ISLANDS

In the Caribbean Sea lies a chain of tropical islands that stretch for 2,000 miles down to the coast of South America. The islands were colonized in the 16th century by Europeans, who brought over African slaves to work plantations. Today, these islands form 25 separate countries. The islanders, most of whom are descendants of slaves, mainly depend on tourism and agriculture for their income.

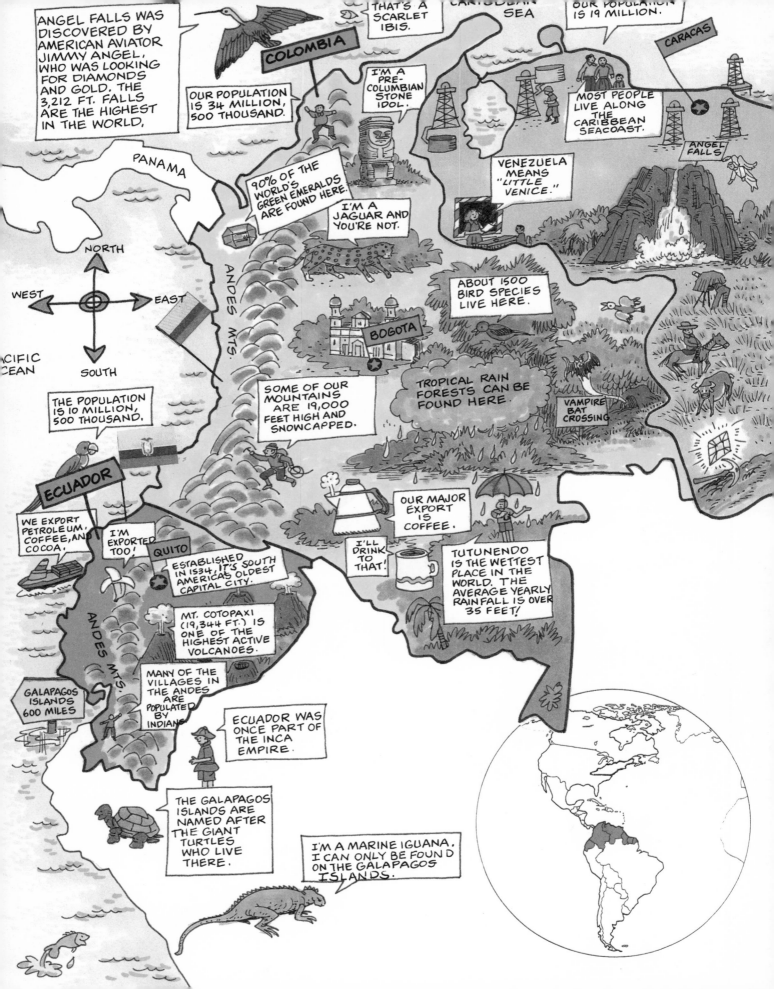

THE NORTHERN COAST
OF SOUTH AMERICA

The northern part of South America is dominated by the Andes Mountains in the west, and by the Amazon forest. The people, like the rest of South America, are of European, Indian, and mixed ancestry.

Find out all about the countries along the northern coast of South America, and where in the world they are. Then look for all the following things, too.

- ☐ Angel
- ☐ Baseball bat
- ☐ Bat
- ☐ Can
- ☐ Cup
- ☐ Emerald
- ☐ Ibis
- ☐ Iguana
- ☐ Jaguar
- ☐ Mountain climber
- ☐ Photographer
- ☐ Satellite rocket
- ☐ Schoolteacher
- ☐ Stone idol
- ☐ Surfer
- ☐ Telescope
- ☐ Turtle

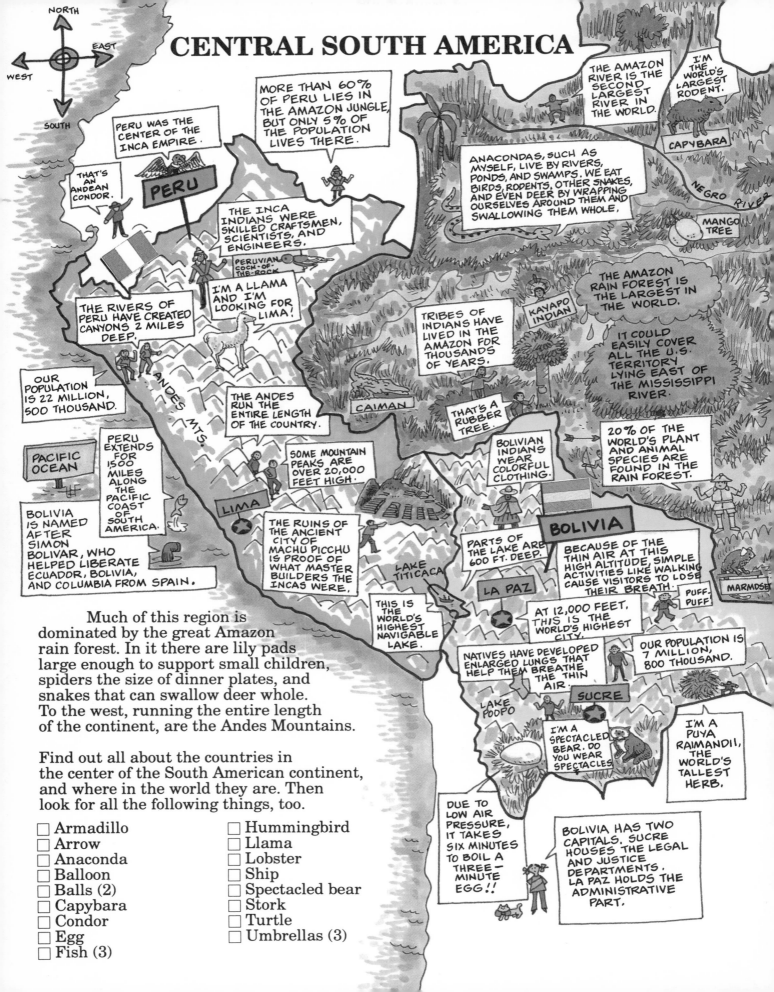

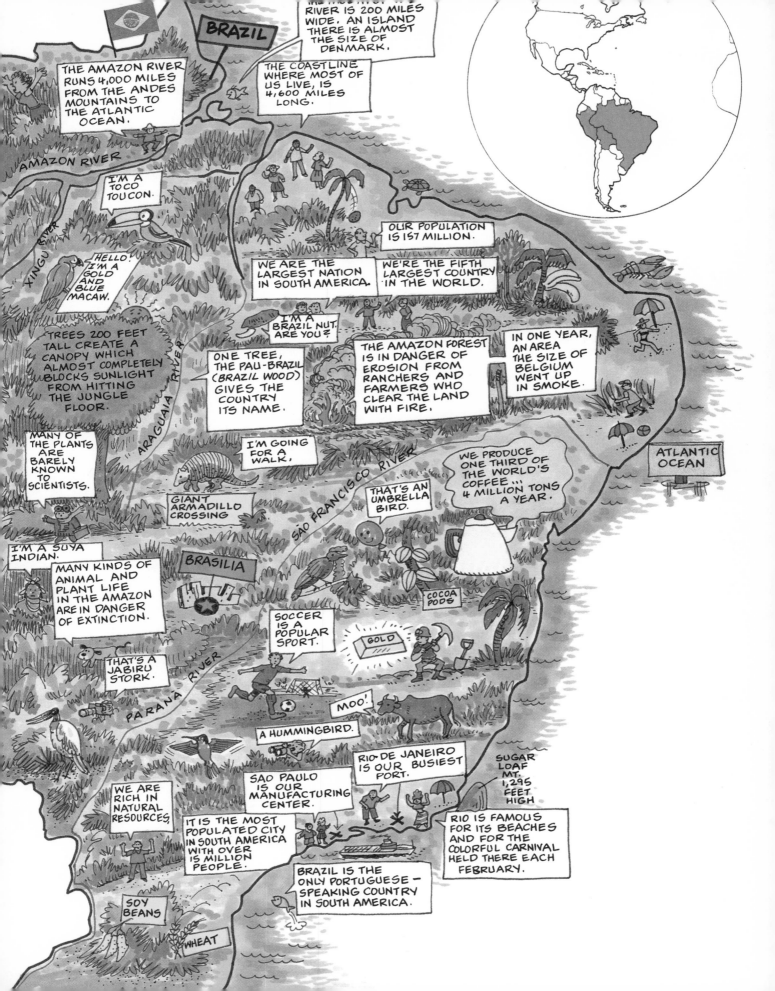

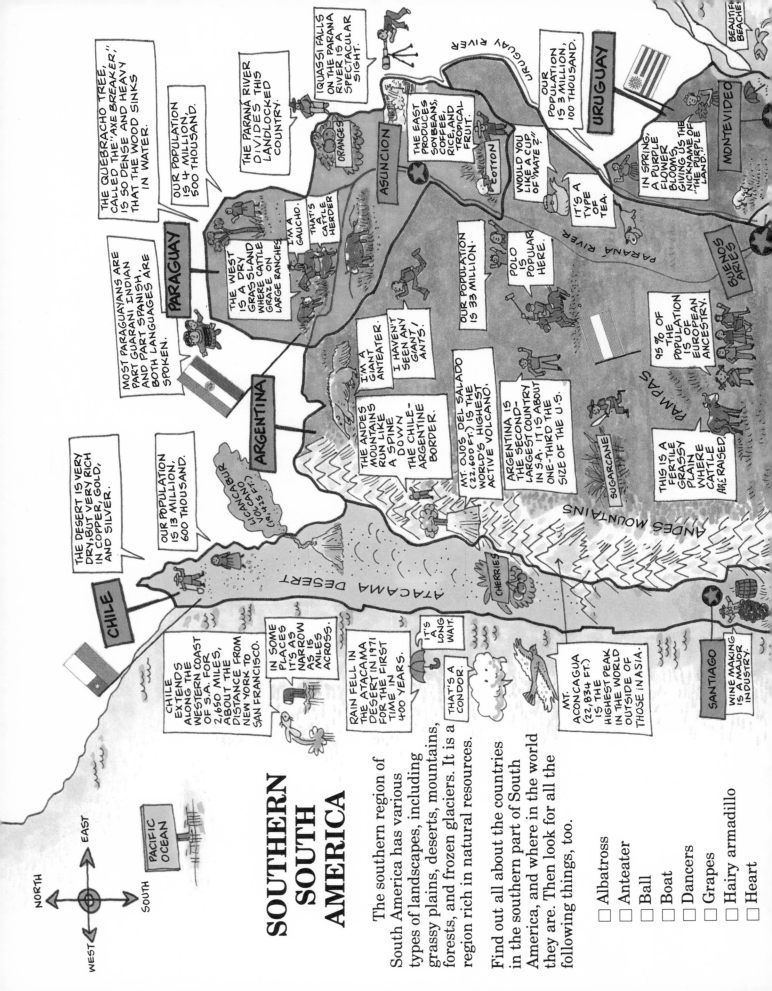

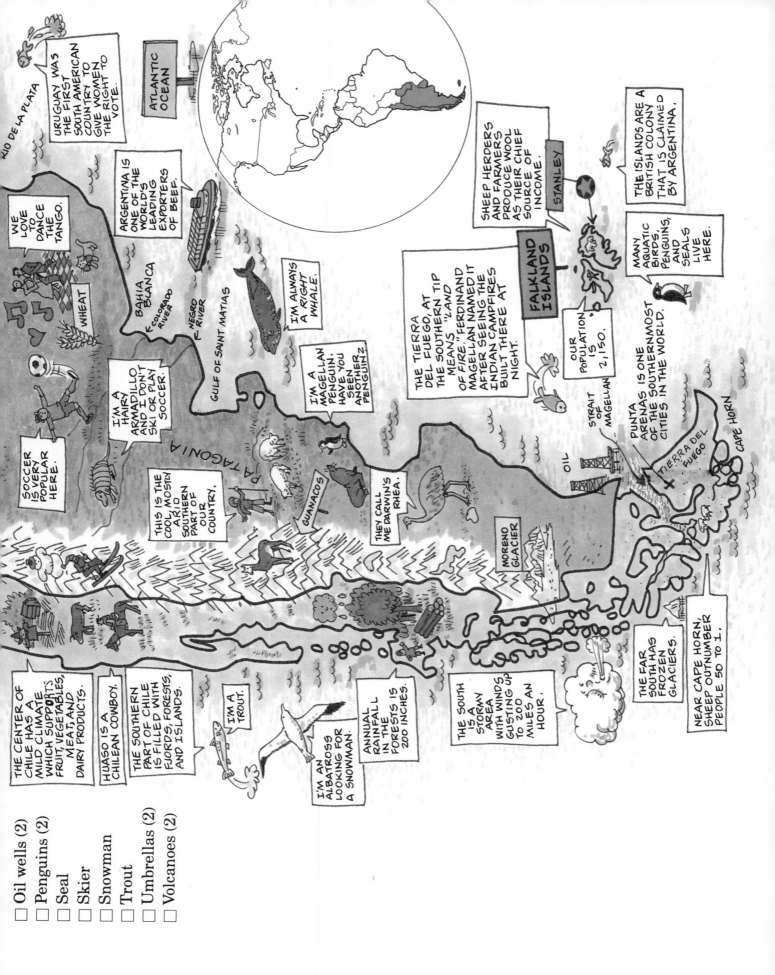

THE UNITED STATES
The Northeast

The most populous region in the country, the northeast was the first to be settled by Europeans. Colonists arrived from England in 1620 and settled New Plymouth, Massachusetts.

Find out all about the northeastern states, and where in the world they are. Then look for all the following things, too.

☐ Anchor
☐ Apple
☐ Baseball
☐ Basketball
☐ Cannon
☐ Kite
☐ Lighthouse
☐ Lobster
☐ Ship
☐ Skier
☐ Treasure chest
☐ Truck
☐ Umbrella

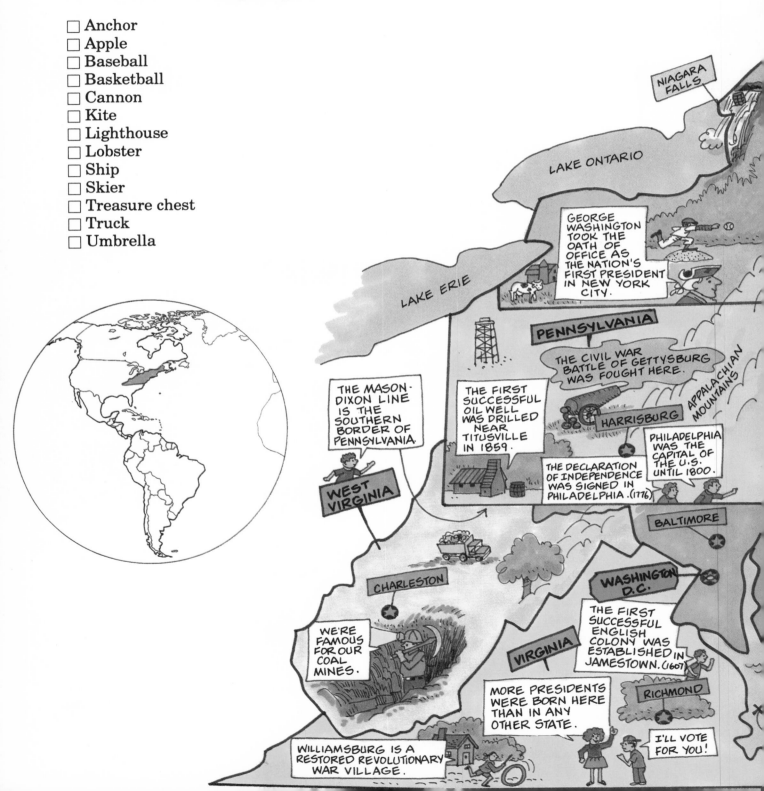

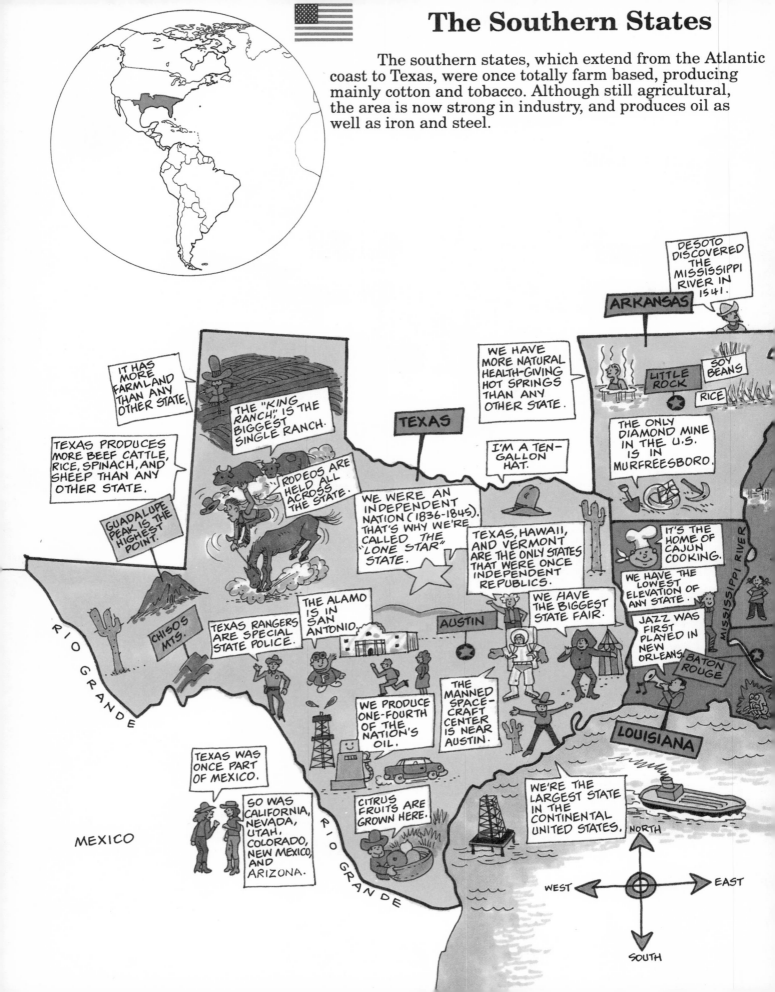

The Southern States

The southern states, which extend from the Atlantic coast to Texas, were once totally farm based, producing mainly cotton and tobacco. Although still agricultural, the area is now strong in industry, and produces oil as well as iron and steel.

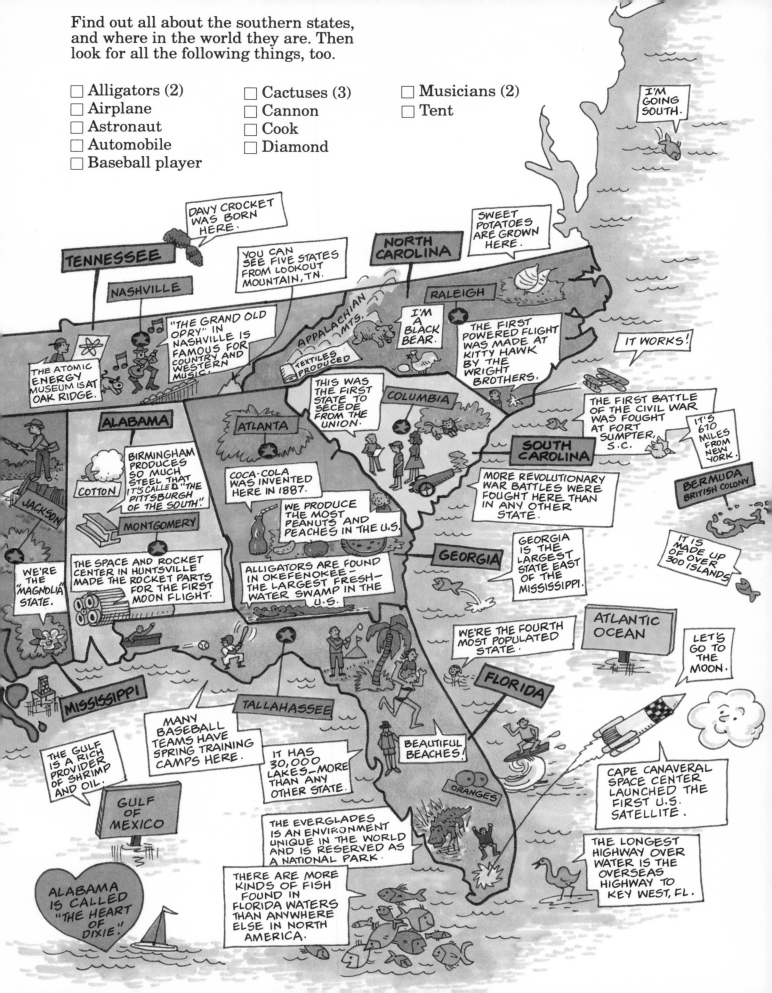

Find out all about the southern states, and where in the world they are. Then look for all the following things, too.

- [ ] Alligators (2)
- [ ] Airplane
- [ ] Astronaut
- [ ] Automobile
- [ ] Baseball player
- [ ] Cactuses (3)
- [ ] Cannon
- [ ] Cook
- [ ] Diamond
- [ ] Musicians (2)
- [ ] Tent

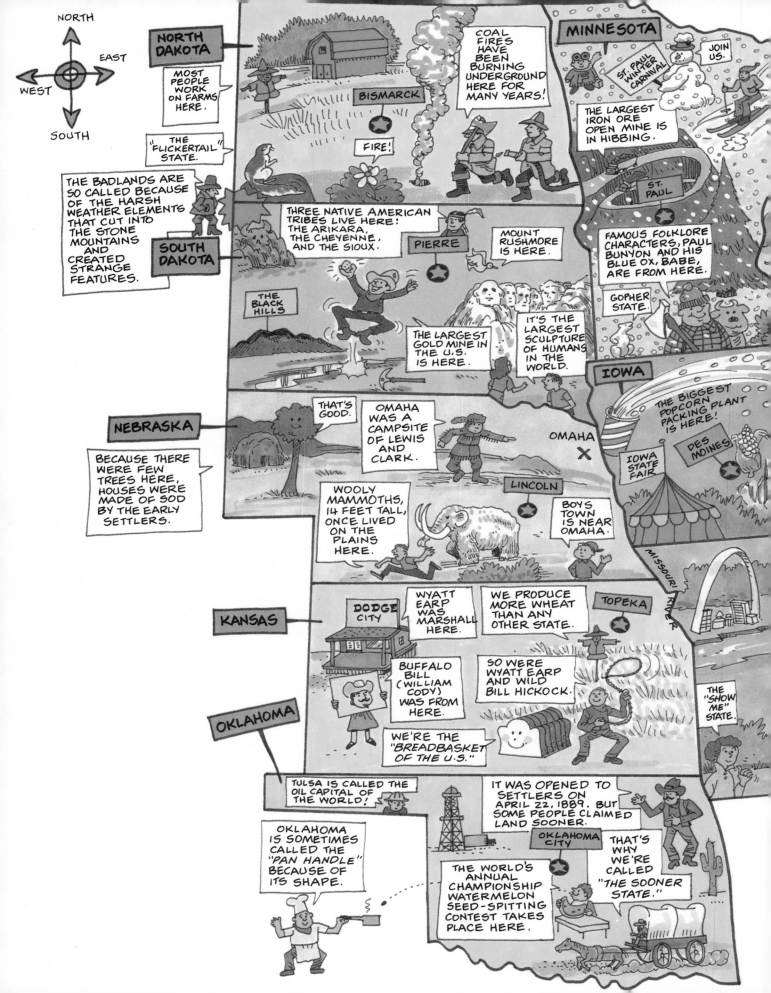

The Midwest

Between the Great Lakes in the north, the Rocky Mountains in the west, and the Appalachians in the east, lies the flat and fertile area known as the Great Plains. The area produces more than half of the world's corn and enough wheat to make the United States the world's largest exporter.

Find out all about the midwestern states, and where in the world they are. Then look for all the following things, too.

- ☐ Blue ox
- ☐ Book
- ☐ Cereal
- ☐ Flower
- ☐ Football
- ☐ Heart
- ☐ Race cars (3)
- ☐ Santa Claus
- ☐ Snowman
- ☐ Tire
- ☐ Watermelon slice
- ☐ Wooly mammoth

The Western States

The western part of the United States is characterized by deserts, mountains, river canyons, and great forests. Separated from the east by the Rocky Mountains, the area was greatly settled and developed mostly after the mid 1880's when the railroads linked the west to the east.

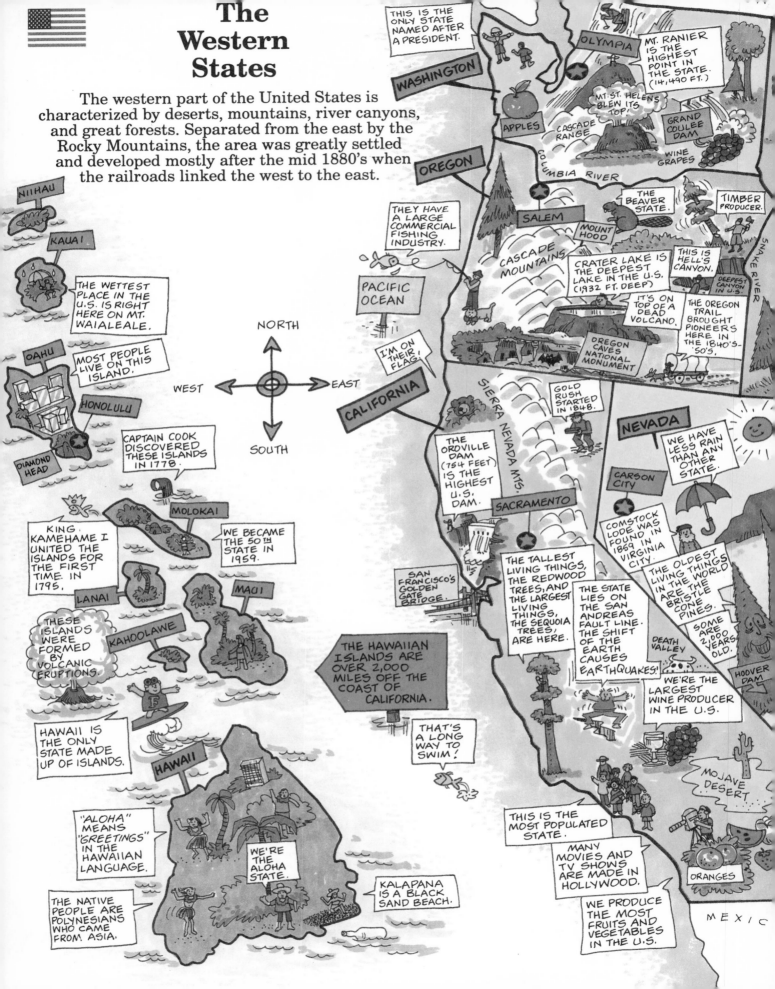

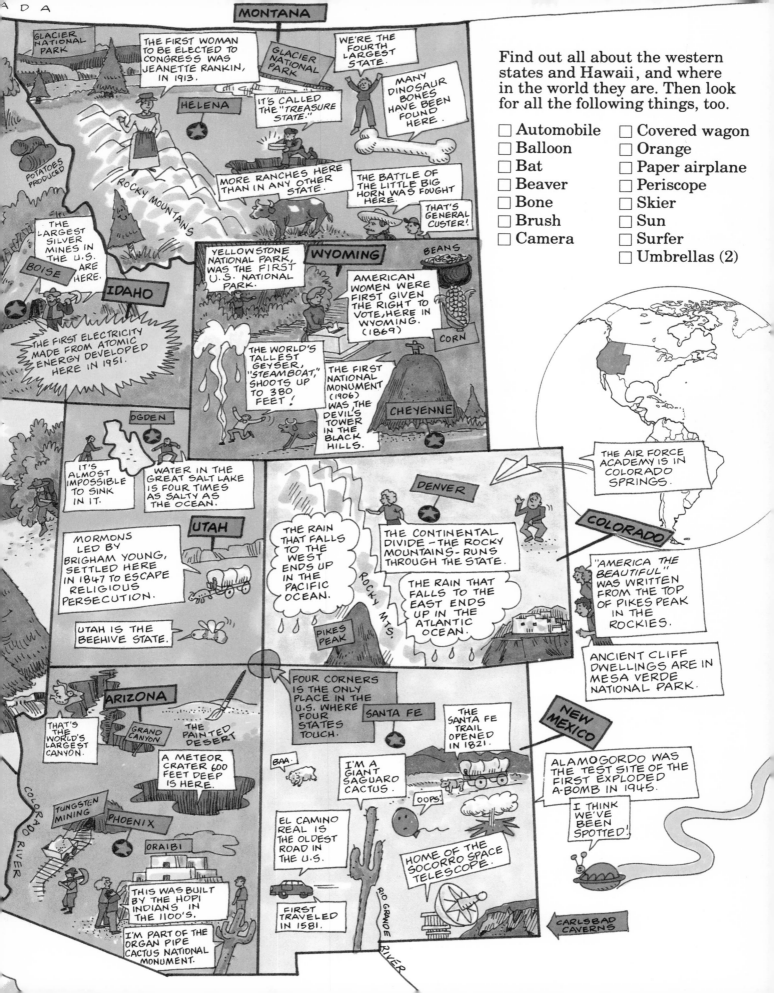

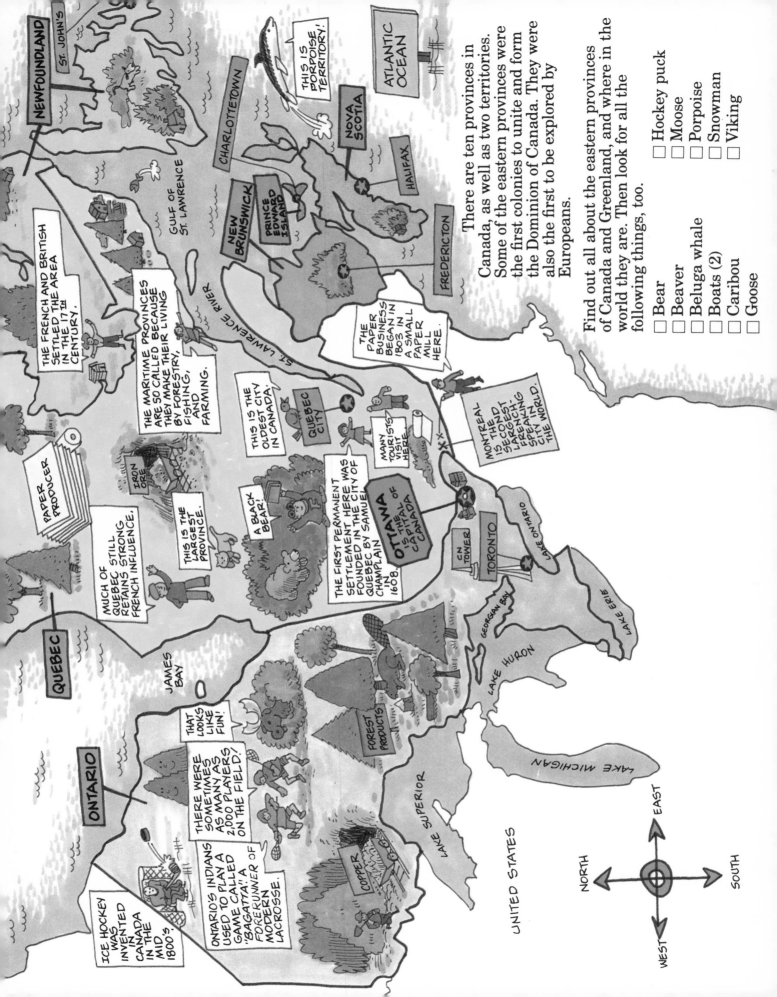

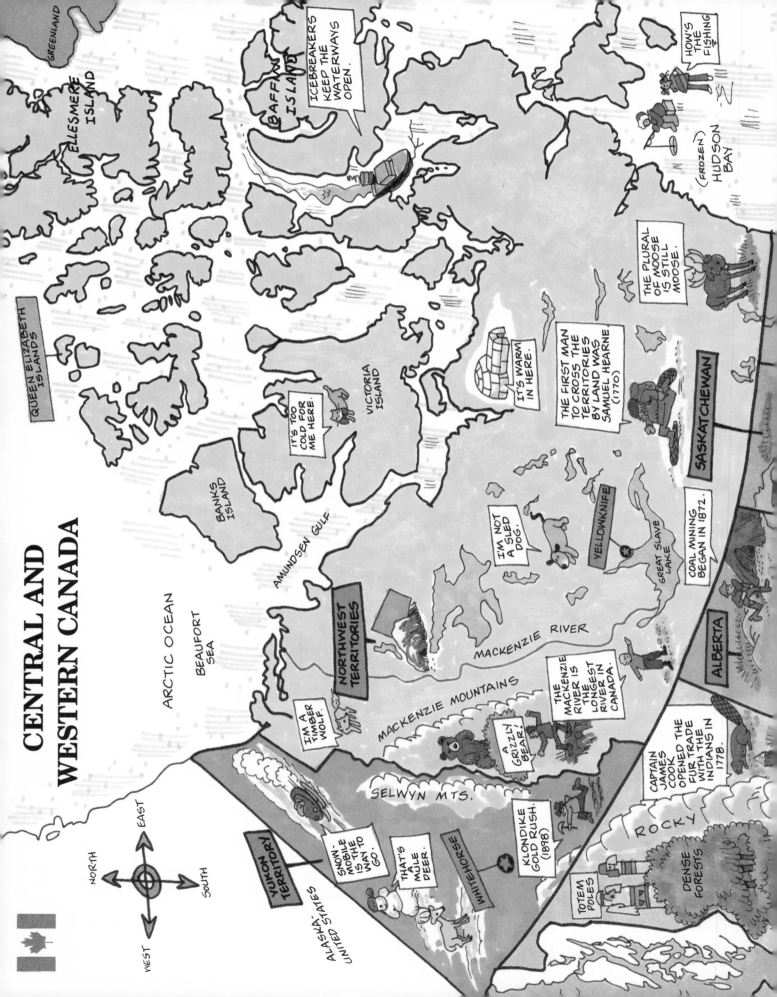

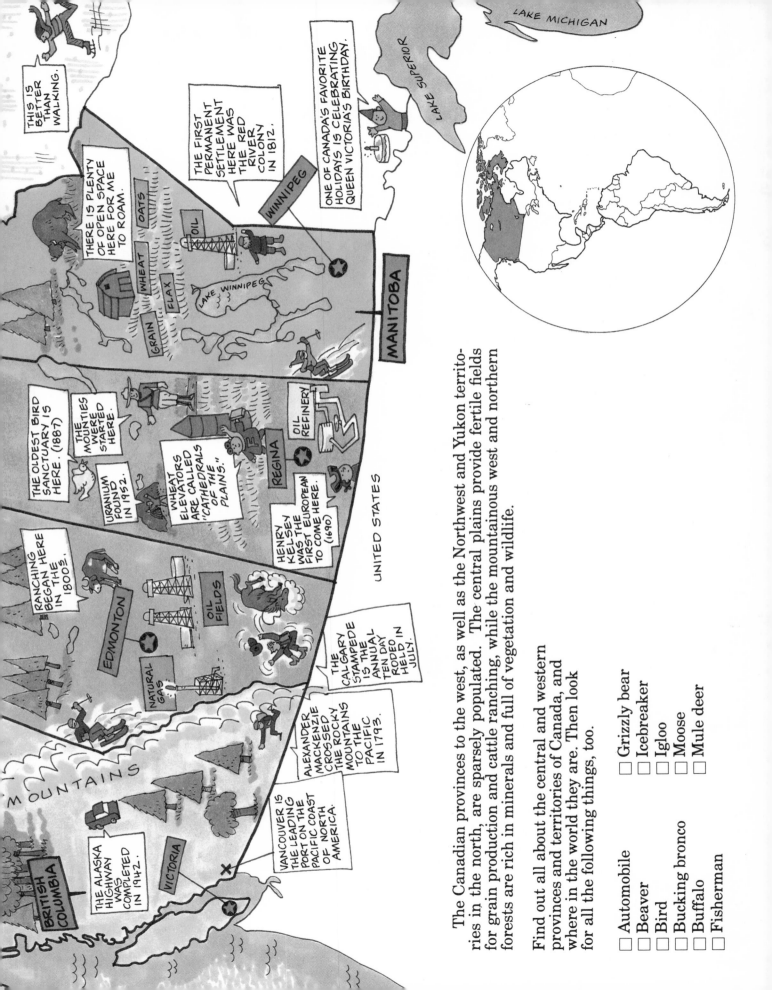

The Canadian provinces to the west, as well as the Northwest and Yukon territories in the north, are sparsely populated. The central plains provide fertile fields for grain production and cattle ranching, while the mountainous west and northern forests are rich in minerals and full of vegetation and wildlife.

Find out all about the central and western provinces and territories of Canada, and where in the world they are. Then look for all the following things, too.

- ☐ Automobile
- ☐ Beaver
- ☐ Bird
- ☐ Bucking bronco
- ☐ Buffalo
- ☐ Fisherman
- ☐ Grizzly bear
- ☐ Icebreaker
- ☐ Igloo
- ☐ Moose
- ☐ Mule deer

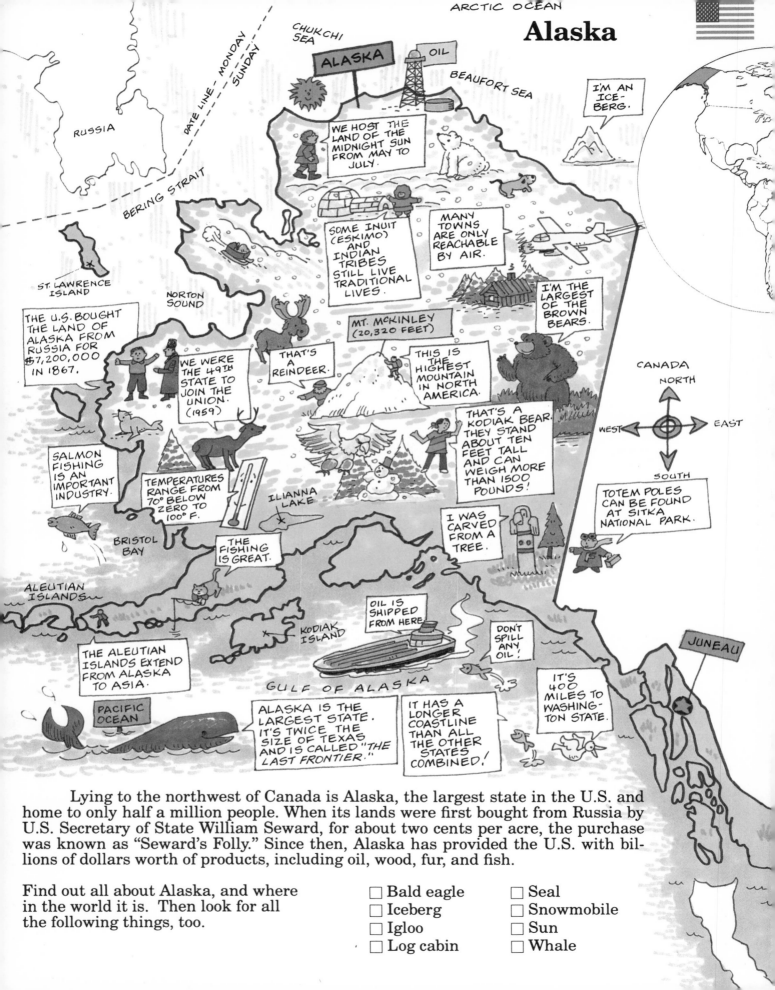

Lying to the northwest of Canada is Alaska, the largest state in the U.S. and home to only half a million people. When its lands were first bought from Russia by U.S. Secretary of State William Seward, for about two cents per acre, the purchase was known as "Seward's Folly." Since then, Alaska has provided the U.S. with billions of dollars worth of products, including oil, wood, fur, and fish.

Find out all about Alaska, and where in the world it is. Then look for all the following things, too.

☐ Bald eagle
☐ Iceberg
☐ Igloo
☐ Log cabin
☐ Seal
☐ Snowmobile
☐ Sun
☐ Whale